I0077040

EMPOWER YOURSELF

A Practical Guide To Connecticut Personal Injury Law

By
Ryan McKeen

Copyright © 2018 Ryan McKeen

All rights reserved. No portion of the book may be reproduced or utilized in any form or by any means, electronic or mechanical, including photocopying, recording, or by any other information storage and retrieval system, without permission in writing from the author.

Table of Contents

Introduction

My first introduction to the legal profession was through a car accident – my own. My girlfriend (now wife) and I had picked up her little brother and we were driving him home. It was a beautiful summer afternoon; our windows were open, and the radio was on. We were traveling at about forty miles per hour when a blue pickup truck took a sudden left out of a gas station. I had no time to react as the driver hit my car near the front right tire, totaling the vehicle. He missed striking the passenger's side door by inches. His wife wasn't wearing a seatbelt and she hit the windshield. We were all lucky to walk away.

In that instant, my life changed. I lost my car, I missed work, and I suffered neck and shoulder pain that continues to this day. After the accident, the insurance company kept calling me and asking questions. I found the process confusing and overwhelming, and I resented that I had been thrust into this situation. I was driving responsibly, but I was the victim of someone else's carelessness and impatience. The best decision I made for myself was to talk to an attorney. He guided me through this process calmly and patiently, and he helped me to resolve my claim. To me, this represents the best of my profession, that an attorney will relieve his or her clients of some of the burden of their troubles so they can focus on healing. This is why I do what I do.

So it's because of this experience that I can say to my clients, "I get it." I understand that while our circumstances may be vastly different, our fear, confusion, and anger is the same. I bring my own experience to bear every time I meet with a new client to discuss their case, from car accident to wrongful death. I recognize that hurt and anxiety in your face, that sense of shock that your life has been suddenly and irrevocably altered. You didn't choose this. You never wanted to wind up in a situation where you're forced to consider a lawsuit to cover your losses and future expenses. I understand.

Like the attorney who inspired me, I want to help you to understand and navigate the often confusing landscape of personal injury law in Connecticut. Armed with this information, your focus can be on healing yourself and your loved ones and moving past the harm that has been done.

I must emphasize that this book is intended to be used as a general resource and that it does not replace or constitute legal advice. If you are a client of mine or of another attorney, some of what you read in this book may conflict with advice you have been given. You should always raise any questions with your attorney, who will take the unique facts of your case into account and advise you accordingly. Finally, legal ethics require that I clarify that this book does not give rise to an attorney-client relationship.

I hope that you find this resource helpful. If you have been injured, I wish you healing, strength, and brighter days ahead.

The Basics

There is a game that's often played at networking events called "Two Truths and a Lie." The idea is that you tell a group of strangers or coworkers three statements about yourself, pretend all three are facts, and see if anyone can pick out the lie. Everyone has a good laugh, and by the end of the game, you know some interesting and maybe even embarrassing details about your new acquaintances. Separating the lies – false first impressions, inherent biases, etc. – to get at the truth of the individual before you seems like a reasonable place to begin any new relationship. So let's start by playing a version of Two Truths and a Lie with the practice of personal injury, which is subject to a great deal of misunderstanding, confusion, and public bias.

LIE #1: Bad things only happen to people who deserve it.

We like to think that we're in control of our lives, and that if we're good people who do the right thing, we can avoid tragedy. It's human nature to see a victim and to think, *If only she had not done X, then Y wouldn't have happened.* This makes us feel safer. We think, *As long as I don't do X, I will never experience Y.*

But the uncomfortable truth is that bad things happen to good, law-abiding folks every day, through no fault of their own. I see it all the time in my practice. So if you're reading this book because something terrible has happened to you or someone you love, let me say this: I don't care what you're telling yourself or what other people are saying, but this is not your fault. You didn't deserve this because no one deserves to be hurt, period.

If you're like most of my clients, you will continue to wrestle with feelings of guilt. It's difficult to accept that something bad happened even though you did everything right. I encourage you to address any such feelings with a trusted counselor because accepting the truth of your circumstances is crucial to healing. Certainly if you are one of my clients and we are heading to trial, I want to talk about these feelings with you. It's crucial to understand the reality of what happened, and why, and to not fall into the trap of blaming the victim – whether it's yourself or someone you love. If you never read past this paragraph, this is what I want you to know. It's that important.

LIE #2: I can't afford to speak with a lawyer about my case.

Lots of times clients call my office, tell me that they've experienced a terrible injury, and then express concern that they don't have the money to hire me. Let's put this lie to bed right now. Most personal injury lawyers – myself included – don't get paid unless and until we recover something for our clients. Our fees are set forth in a written agreement with our client, discussed at the outset of the case, and paid only if we recover. In other words, if you've been injured, you should never be charged for sitting down with an attorney to discuss your case. Ever.

LIE #3: Personal injury lawyers are greedy / ambulance chasers / unethical, etc.

I represent people who have been hurt or sometimes killed, and I usually represent them against powerful insurance companies. Would you believe me if I told you that the insurance companies are the ones who spread this lie because they want you to distrust your own lawyer?

Let me tell you what my job entails. I sit with injured or grieving people and try to understand their pain. I take on their burden of speaking with claims adjusters or the police so they can focus on healing. I fight like hell for them, navigating them through a confusing, often hostile system. Whether we agree to settle or ultimately take a jury verdict, I spend months and often years trying to get my clients whatever they need to be made whole again in the eyes of the law.

I guess this one is a matter of opinion, so you'll have to form your own. But the lawyers I know who represent injured individuals are some of my most ethical and courageous colleagues. They stand – often all alone – against multibillion-dollar corporations in order to protect the powerless. In spite what the public at large may believe about us, I'm honored to be a part of this group and to represent individuals.

So there you have it, a few insidious lies. Allow me to highlight the truth:

TRUTH #1: You didn't deserve what happened to you or your loved one.

TRUTH #2: You can afford to speak with me or a colleague.

TRUTH #3: If I take your case, I'm darn proud and honored to represent you.

Thank you for indulging me in this get-to-know-you game. Now let's get to the substance of this book, which is you.

The Beginning

The dog wakes you up early Sunday morning. You throw on sandals and take her outside to the spot – you know, the one place on the planet the dog finds suitable to do her business. Still half asleep, you come back inside and make coffee.

The kids are awake. They want Honey Nut Cheerios and cartoons. You turn on the television for them, which buys about 30 minutes of quiet before they want something else.

You check the sports scores on your phone and then look through the kitchen for your own breakfast. There's nothing to eat—well, aside from Honey Nut Cheerios, but the kids have been eating them directly from the box and who knows where those hands have been. You decide to go to the store and pick up eggs and bagels.

You gently nudge your still-sleeping spouse. "Honey, sleep in. The kids are watching Netflix and I'm going to get bagels. The dog has gone out. I'll be back soon."

You get in your car, back out of your driveway, and adjust the radio. Sunday morning radio is kind of sad. No station has a live host. You decide to play whatever CD is in your car CD player. You hope it's not Kidz Bop.

Then it happens. The only thing you remember is the noise. That terrible sound.

You wake up in the hospital. You don't know what happened. You don't know what day it is. Everything hurts – bad. Your first thought is for your family. Are they okay?

Alarms go off. Nurses run in. You hear them say, "He's come to."

You struggle to speak and they tell you to relax. Sometime later your wife comes in the room. You know it's her. You recognize her cry. "The kids are okay," she says. "Everything is going to be okay." But you both know everything is the opposite of okay.

There's all the medical stuff. They're talking about stabilizing you, then they're talking about moving you to a rehab facility. Moving anything seems impossible. Everything is broken.

Then there's everything left behind. Who is going to take the dog out? Who is going to get the kids cereal? Who is going to mow the lawn? How are you going to pay the bills? Will you ever be able to go back to work?

Your life has turned on a dime.

Slowly, you come to understand what happened. Your car was hit by a truck while the driver was texting. And before you're even discharged from the hospital, the truck company wants your statement. But how can you give a statement? You only remember the sound. You wonder if you have to give this statement at all, especially while you still feel groggy.

Does my insurance pay for this? Who pays for this?

You need help, but you don't know where to turn. It seems every time you turn on the TV to distract yourself from the pain, another ad for a personal attorney is on. You never imagined you'd be in a position to need a personal injury attorney. Do you trust your family's future to the guy on TV?

You know the choices you and your wife make in these early days are going to shape everything going forward. You hope to make the right choices. You **need** to make the right choices. Where do you turn?

This is just the beginning.

***

Tragedy comes in many forms. Maybe you experienced a car accident like the driver in my hypothetical. Or maybe you were injured as a passenger or as a guest at someone's home. Or maybe you a call letting you know that someone you love was not coming home. Each of these tragedies sets a person on a slightly different path through the legal landscape, but there are some basic commonalities that we'll discuss here.

1. Do I need a lawyer?

My clients experience a great deal of fear and uncertainty at the outset. They are shocked and hurt, both emotionally and physically. When the dust begins to settle, they ask themselves whether they need to speak with a lawyer.

It's important to note that in Connecticut, personal injury lawyers are ethically prohibited from soliciting clients. A lawyer should never contact you first, so please don't assume that you don't have a good case because a lawyer hasn't called you. That's simply not how it works. In any personal injury action, the first step is a phone call from the client to an attorney.

I know how it is in the Age of Google. You can spend days on the internet researching your own legal position and coming to your own conclusion. But internet advice is dubious at best. You really need someone to evaluate your particular set of facts against their real-life legal experience and the laws of your state. We've already dispelled the myth that you need to have lots of money before you hire a personal injury lawyer, and in some cases, if you hesitate too long, you may miss early filing deadlines your lawyer needs to meet to keep your case alive. So when you start to question whether you have a case, my advice is to pick up the phone sooner rather than later.

As a lawyer, I consider it an honor to get that phone call, and I answer the phone most hours of the day or night. I do what I do because I like helping people. If you call me and I don't think you have a legal case, I may still be able to give you some direction as to how to proceed. For example, I may tell you that you have a case, but that it's something you can handle without my assistance. Or I might refer you to a trusted colleague whom I believe is better suited to help you. Oftentimes, I'll set up a meeting with a potential client to discuss the case in greater detail and decide on the best approach together. Of course, if I don't think you have a case, that's only my judgment based on my experience. If you disagree, then by all means call someone else.

Whatever happens, you should feel better after simply making that first phone call and getting more information.

2. How do I choose a lawyer?

This is a big decision. You're choosing someone to represent your interests, and the firm you pick may be with you for years. Here are a few things to keep in mind.

As the client, you are in charge. Always. You can interview as many law firms as you'd like before making a decision. If you get into a bad relationship, you can terminate your retainer agreement and hire a different lawyer. I recommend doing your research at the outset. Make a few phone calls, take a few meetings, and get a sense of some different styles and levels of experience. Ask yourself if you're comfortable asking this lawyer a question, especially one that you worry may seem foolish. Is this lawyer friendly? Cold? Professional? Sloppy? Trust your gut here.

Unfortunately, some lawyers rely on high-pressure sales tactics to retain clients. In my experience it's not the norm, but it can happen. If you attend a meeting with a lawyer who tries to pressure you into signing with them right away, remember that you're the one in charge. You shouldn't do anything that makes you feel uncomfortable.

Not all lawyers practice in personal injury. The practice of law has grown increasingly complex over the years. More and more, general practice firms are vanishing and so-called "boutique" firms with a narrow focus are replacing them. It's not that lawyers don't want to be the first call for all your basic legal needs anymore. We focus because we owe our clients the duty of competence, and the legal landscape has become too complicated for most attorneys to competently practice in multiple, unrelated practice areas.

I speak from experience here. When I started practicing, I worked in a general practice firm. I was representing clients in simple real estate transactions, business disputes, and divorce – sometimes all on the same day. The variety kept life interesting, but as I matured as a professional, I decided that I wanted to do more of what I loved. That's why I made a conscious choice to devote my entire practice to understanding the complexities of personal injury law. And trust me, it can be complex. I regularly attend conferences and classes on topics as diverse as jury psychology and traumatic brain injury. This focus means that I have the knowledge and support to competently handle a spectrum of injury cases, from minor car accidents to wrongful death. Many of my colleagues who practice in personal injury devote a large part of their practice to personal injury, as well.

It's important for you to keep all this in mind when you start making calls. Interview your lawyer (remember, you're in charge). Ask her whether she has experience in personal injury matters like your own. Ask him what percentage of his practice is devoted to personal injury. Try to determine whether this is an attorney who can best serve your needs. This advice seems obvious if you have experienced a tragic event as complicated as a medical malpractice or a wrongful death, but any personal injury case may be more complicated than it initially appears. I've personally taken on seemingly minor car accident cases that became much more complicated when the victim discovered he was suffering from neurological damage as a result. If your case heats up, you want to make sure you've retained a lawyer who knows how to handle it. If you haven't, it's time to make a switch.

Not all lawyers go to court. When you think of lawyers, you probably think of the courtroom. That's what's on television and in the movies, after all. But in reality, very few lawyers routinely appear in court these days. Any lawyer is able to appear in court, of course, but not all of them do. As discussed above, there are many kinds of law and many different ways to practice.

If you have a personal injury case, your lawyer has to prepare for trial. In my opinion, this is not optional. Even if your case ultimately settles, you want an attorney who is ready and willing to go before a jury. You want an attorney who is not afraid to take a verdict.

These days, the vast majority of personal injury cases settle before they reach trial. As I'll discuss, there are many factors that come into play here, not the least of which is the uncertainty of a jury trial. But even so, you probably want a lawyer who has had the experience of trying a case and taking a jury verdict. Why? Because you want a lawyer who knows how to gather evidence, hire and interview experts, and be tough with insurance companies when they aren't offering fair compensation. You want a lawyer who's been there, done that.

I've had cases settle after we sent the first demand letter. I've also had cases settle at jury selection, or on the first day of trial, right before I make my opening statement. I've been forced to take cases to verdict when an insurance company won't be reasonable. In each of those instances, I would have short-changed my clients if I hadn't been fully ready to try their case. Ask any lawyer you interview whether they have taken a jury verdict and whether they are prepared to try your case if necessary. You may be surprised at how difficult this experience is to find these days.

3. What else should I ask a prospective lawyer?

I've made some interview suggestions above, but if I were looking for an attorney, there are a couple of additional key questions I would ask.

First, do you have legal malpractice insurance? Ask this question. I have done hundreds if not thousands of potential client interviews, but I have never been asked about my insurance. In Connecticut, lawyers are not required to carry legal malpractice insurance. They're also not required to disclose that they don't insure. However, lawyers can commit legal malpractice in a variety of ways. Some common ways to commit malpractice are by failing to file a lawsuit within the statute of limitations period or by failing to give a proper, legally required notice. Lawyers can also commit malpractice by wrongfully settling your case. Make no mistake: legal malpractice insurance protects clients.

Second, do you conduct focus groups? At Connecticut Trial Firm, we don't guess how a jury may respond to our case. We ask. In a focus group format, we speak with randomly selected potential jurors – in other words, area residents over the age of eighteen who could be called to jury duty in the court in which we are trying a case. We discuss our case with the focus group, and their questions and opinions give us insight into our case's strengths and weaknesses. We have invested a lot of time and resources into running an effective and cost-efficient focus group practice. The focus groups we conduct don't add thousands of dollars to the expense ledger in your case, but they have made a big impact in our cases. We have found them to be an invaluable research tool. So when you interview a lawyer, I encourage you to ask him or her whether they engage in this practice. If they do, ask them how much their focus groups cost.

4. How do I use this book?

Once again, this book is not legal advice or a substitute for an attorney.

I don't expect you to read this book from cover to cover, though you are welcome to do so. Instead, I encourage you to skip around and read the chapters that apply to your case. Make notes, use a highlighter, fold page corners – do whatever you do – and use this book as a starting point for further discussion with your attorney. The legal process can be a challenging one – intimidating, frustratingly slow, and downright puzzling at times. I want to remove some of the mystique and give you the general landscape of different legal actions so you are prepared for the road ahead.

5. One last point...

I use the terms "lawyer" and "attorney" interchangeably throughout the book. In Connecticut, they have the same meaning and refer to someone who is admitted to practice at the bar.

An Introduction to Personal Injury Law

You're driving down the highway. It's raining. You need to take your daughter to Target to get a bathing suit, and once in Target you know you won't leave without buying a dozen other things that you forgot you needed. You are minding your business and staying in lane.

Then you look in your rearview mirror and see the eighteen-wheeler behind you. It's far too close. And then you hear the truck's air brakes and feel a bump. Your car fishtails. Suddenly you are sideways and being pushed by a Mack truck down the highway. This goes on for what feels like an eternity.

Your daughter shrieks, "Daddy, are we going to be okay?"

She is panicking, and you instinctively reassure her, "Yes, honey." But you know full well that if your wheel catches, your car will roll and your wife will lose both her husband and her daughter.

By the grace of God, the truck and your car comes to a stop. Your windows are blown out. Your car has heavy damage. But you didn't roll. You are alive. You are "okay."

When you post about it on Facebook you write, "We were in an accident but we're okay." By "okay" you mean you're not dead. The muscles in your neck continue to spasm, and you hit your head on the window. You hurt in places you didn't know you had. Your car is totaled.

You go to the hospital. They do X-rays, say nothing is broken, give you some prescription muscle relaxants, and tell you to contact your doctor. You do. Your doctor recommends you go for physical therapy. Your bills are being paid by your health insurance. You have some co-pays, but fortunately they are manageable.

All things considered, you're lucky. Insurance helps you pay for a rental car and gets you prompt payment, which allows you to get a new car. You're not a lawsuit guy. You see the lawyers on TV and know that people milk claims to get money they don't deserve. You're not that guy. You go to work even though it hurts.

Your friend says, "You should really talk to a lawyer about this." You initially dismiss the idea, but your headaches persist and your daughter experiences terrible nightmares. Over time, you begin to think that maybe you should speak to someone after all.

What is the purpose of personal injury law?

1. Accountability

We all know that conduct rewarded is conduct repeated. Dog owners know this as well as parents do. If you don't correct unwanted behavior, you have essentially rewarded it, and you can be sure you are in for more of that unwanted behavior in the future. The same thing is true for drivers, companies, and insurance companies. If you don't stand up and hold them accountable for bad conduct, it will happen again. Maybe next time someone isn't as lucky as you were. Maybe the next time the above scenario occurs, the tire catches, the car flips, and the car and its occupants are crushed.

Hitting businesses, drivers, and insurance companies in their wallet is the only way to make things safer. It is the only language that big companies understand.

2. Responsibility

You believe in personal responsibility. You live it. You mess up, you 'fess up. You make it right.

We have plenty of safety laws – many of which are written in the blood of those who have died before. Laws are only words. Laws mean nothing unless ordinary folks stand up and insist they are enforced. Our legal system depends on the personal responsibility of citizens to enforce the laws and hold wrongdoers fully accountable.

When you hold a wrongdoer accountable, you may discover what happened to you wasn't just due to a momentary mistake. Maybe the trucking company hired a driver who wasn't qualified. Maybe the company chose not to perform maintenance on the truck. Maybe your accident was fully preventable and attributable to the negligence of the company or driver. You won't know unless you hold the wrongdoer up to the standard you hold yourself to: personal responsibility.

3. Making You Whole

Your daughter shouldn't be having those nightmares.

You shouldn't be losing sleep because you can't get comfortable. And the headaches? They interfere with your job. You grit your teeth and push on. But you did nothing wrong here, so why are you and your family paying the price?

Law is limited by physics and biology, and no court can undo what has been done to you. No court can heal you. All the law can provide you with is money to make up for what has been lost and what you and your daughter have been put through. You're not entitled to more, but you shouldn't accept less. Just having your medical bills paid is not enough. It doesn't make you whole.

Takeaways

Holding wrongdoers accountable and making them take personal responsibility is what our country and legal system are grounded in. We don't do this for fun. Rather, we do this because we know that legal actions are a type of activism. We know that standing up is hard. But when you stand up, the trucking company may change its rules. The driver may put his phone down. Standing up saves lives.

You deserve to be made as whole as the law can make you. The law can't erase your daughter's bad memories, but the trucking company should pay so you have money to create new and positive memories with her.

The only way you hold wrongdoers accountable is by making sure you are made whole.

What could delay the resolution of my case?

Personal injury attorneys commonly advertise on TV (we don't). The ads can be boiled down to "Call us and get money fast" – as if being in a car wreck or losing a dear loved one is like drawing a winning scratch ticket from the local gas station.

This kind of advertising sickens me. It benefits no one but the marketers pushing the ads. It creates an unrealistic expectation that personal injury cases are easy and quick money. This expectation gets used against seriously injured folks by juries. Some Connecticut defense attorneys even go so far as improperly arguing in closing that the case is about the plaintiff trying to hit the lottery. Nothing can be further from the truth.

Injury cases can take months or even years to resolve, and this is most unfortunate. Insurance companies make money on claims. They know you are out of work. They know you have lost a loved one whose income you relied on to support your family. They know you are getting bills from hospital debt collectors. They know you are worrying about paying your mortgage or sending in that money for your daughter's field trip. They know it and they like it. No matter how nice an adjuster may seem, know that he or she is a paid corporate shill working at the direction of big money to boost stock price for some insurance company so that overpaid executives can get their obscene bonuses. Make no mistake, that is what you are facing.

Years ago, insurance companies adopted a strategy called "Delay, Deny, and Defend" in regards to handling claims. They know that time is on their side. They don't worry about paying their medical bills. They know that the longer they keep you from the money you are owed, the more desperate you will become. In fact, they hope that you will get mad at your attorney or the courts, because they know when you're mad and you're desperate, you'll take pennies on the dollar.

So with that big picture in mind, here are five reasons your personal injury claim may take time to resolve:

1. You Are Not Done with Treatment

Aside from insurance company tactics, this is one of the single biggest reasons cases take time to resolve. Once you sign a release, you can never come back and ask for more money. If you sign a release on day one and on day two the doctor tells you that you need a hip replacement as a result of the car accident, then you're out of luck. You are on the hook for the entire tab. Injury cases should only be settled when you are done with treatment or when your treating doctor believes you have reached maximum medical improvement and has written down what your future care will be and how much it will cost.

2. There Is a Real Dispute in Your Case

Maybe the other guy says the light was red and you swear it was green. Your lawyer has the responsibility to prove your case. Proving a case can take time. Often, written documents like police reports and hospital bills will not be enough to prove a case. There will have to be depositions (out-of-court sworn testimony) and expert investigations before parties can evaluate their risks of trial.

Disputes sometimes arise as to how something happened, how injured a person is, and whether or not the defendant caused your injuries.

3. There Are Legal Issues In Your Personal Injury Case

In addition to factual disputes, sometimes lawyers disagree about the law. This will cause the parties to file motions. A motion is a paper filed with the court requesting that the judge take a certain action. For example, a motion to strike is a request for the judge to remove—or strike—something in a complaint because the moving party believes this element of the complaint is improper. There are many kinds of motions and each is a little different, but they really seek to do the same thing: determine how the law applies to a case. Motions can be complicated and multiple motions may be filed. It may take time to write legal briefs (essays to assist the judge in making a decision) on your behalf. Once a case is argued, judges have four months to issue a ruling. The wheels of justice can turn slowly.

4. Your Lawyer Isn't Working Your Case

Lawyers have to gather information, but lawyers get busy. Your lawyer should keep you informed every step of the way. If you haven't heard from your lawyer in a while, check in with them.

5. Records are delayed

In Connecticut, the police have a year to put together a report on an accident. Sometimes, in complicated and catastrophic accidents, it takes them every last second of that year to issue a report. Additionally, even once a report is issued it may take months—in some departments in Connecticut, as long as six months – for the police to give it to you. Even the most diligent lawyer can't do anything without the report.

Sometimes medical providers take forever to produce records, despite repeated requests. There is nothing an attorney can do. We need those records to settle and evaluate your case.

Conclusion

You and your lawyer should have an ongoing conversation about how long your case will take. Every case is different. Some hospitals turn over records quickly, others do not. Some cases don't involve complicated legal issues and filing motions isn't necessary or expected. Other cases may result in appeals to higher courts, which can take years. You should never be afraid to ask your lawyer approximately how long your case will take, and when you do so, understand that the best you can hope for is that your attorney moves your case forward as quickly as possible.

Be wary of any lawyer who promises quick money. Quick money is likely short money.

How do I evaluate cases?

When I meet with injured people, I am often asked, "Do I have a case?"

The answer requires a knowledge of the law, an investigation of the claim, and an understanding of the prospective client's situation. Every case is different. Only an experienced personal injury attorney can answer this question.

When prospective clients come to me, I always ask myself two questions: (1) What do I have to prove? and (2) Can I prove it? To answer these questions, I think about the civil burden of proof, which is commonly referred to as a preponderance standard. Below I've paraphrased and cut from the Connecticut Civil Jury Instructions on burden of proof:

In civil cases, an injured person who asserts a claim has the burden of proving it by a fair preponderance of the evidence. That is, the better or weightier evidence must establish that, more probably than not, the assertion is true.

In weighing the evidence, a jury must keep in mind that it is the quality and not the quantity of evidence that is important. One piece of believable evidence may weigh so heavily as to overcome a multitude of less credible evidence. The weight to be accorded each piece of evidence is for the jury to decide.

Imagine the scales of justice. Put all the credible evidence on the scale. If the scales incline, even slightly, in favor of the assertion, then may you find the assertion has been proved by a fair preponderance of the evidence.

The preponderance standard in personal injury cases is much different from the "beyond a reasonable doubt" standard in criminal cases. In a criminal case, the prosecutor has to prove to a judge or jury that there is no reasonable doubt as to whether the accused committed the crime in question. That's a very heavy burden, and rightly so. In a personal injury case, however, we simply have to prove that our version of the facts is more likely than not. For example, we will say that the motor vehicle accident in question only occurred because the defendant engaged in bad conduct, such as texting while driving. If you think about certainty on a scale of 1 to 100%, we must convince the judge or jury to a point just above 50% certainty. It's not beyond a reasonable doubt, but more like, "Yeah, it probably happened that way."

When I evaluate a case, I ask myself whether we can convince a jury or trial judge that what happened to you most likely occurred as a result of the defendant's bad conduct. If I think we can, then I'll tell you that I think you have a case.

Case evaluation is more art than science, of course, and reasonable minds may differ. This is why I always encourage prospective clients to speak with another attorney if I turn away their case. At the end of the day, case evaluation is based solely on my professional judgment and experience.

What is a personal injury?

That's a question a lot of folks have. There are all sorts of commercials on TV that say, "Injured? Call me!" The billboards line our highways. It seems every third ad on the radio is for a personal injury lawyer, but the term "personal injury" is a little confusing.

There are lots of kinds of injuries. You may be walking and stub your toe on the way to the bathroom. You may hit your funny bone on a doorway. And there can be even more serious injuries than those – you are working on your house and fall off a ladder. None of the commercials or ads explain which of these injuries is considered a personal injury. They just want you to call. But calling can be awkward. No one wants to be sold. Sometimes people aren't ready to hire a lawyer, they just want more information.

When these ads are talking about injuries or personal injuries, they are really talking about *compensable* injuries: someone else has done something wrong and as a result, you are hurt. So my example about walking into the door frame and hurting your funny bone is not a compensable bodily injury – there's no one to blame but you.

Here are some kinds of personal injuries that are compensable in Connecticut:

A Car Accident

Someone is not paying attention and hits your car. The collision is violent and causes damages to both you and your car. Car accidents commonly result in compensable injuries.

A Dog Bite or Animal Attack

Dog owners and keepers are fully accountable for dog bites. In Connecticut, sometimes landlords can be held accountable for a dog bite.

Legal, Medical, and Dental Malpractice

"Malpractice" is a fancy word for a professional being held accountable for things they did wrong – things that violate the rules of their profession— such as a lawyer missing a statute of limitations or a doctor operating on the wrong leg.

Premises Liability

Premises liability holds property owners accountable for defects on their property that injure others. These defects can be snow and ice, not broken stairs, inadequate security, or damaged sidewalks and driveways.

A Bike or Pedestrian Accident

Riding a bike or going for a walk can be dangerous. Cars are often going too fast, and drivers are distracted by cell phones. Unfortunately, pedestrians and cyclists are the most likely to be injured as distracted drivers don't see them until it is too late. Pedestrian and bike accidents often have serious consequences.

A Motorcycle Accident

Like bikes and pedestrians, motorcycles are especially vulnerable on the roads. Drivers simply don't pay attention, and in an accident, it is the motorcyclist who gets hurt.

A Trucking Accident

Connecticut has a lot of big rigs on its highways. As retailers look to move goods between Boston and New York, sometimes trucking companies take shortcuts on maintaining their trucks, training their employees, and complying with trucking law. These rule violations often have severe consequences.

Assault or Sexual Abuse

Sometimes people do terrible things to each other, including assault or sexual abuse. The wrongdoers can be held both civilly and criminally liable for their actions.

Wrongful Death

Death is the ultimate injury. Wrongful death claims arise from car accidents, malpractice, dog bites, motorcycle accidents, pedestrian accidents, premises defects, and assaults.

Takeaways

Those are the main categories of personal injuries in Connecticut, though there may be other kinds of injuries as well. The only way to know if you have a case is to consult with a personal injury attorney.

What is the process you follow in a personal injury case?

We're often asked at initial meetings with clients what the process is in a personal injury case. At Connecticut Trial Firm we have a seven-step proven process that we employ in all our personal injury cases.

1. Listen

Listening is always the first step. Our first mission is to understand what happened, what you are going through, and how your life has changed. In order to understand, we listen. Listening allows us to explain your situation to an adjuster, opposing counsel, a mediator, a judge, and/or a jury. We think it's essential for you to feel like you've been heard.

2. Counsel

Knowledge is power, and we are committed to helping you understand the law in commonsense terms.

3. Investigate

Our team has to investigate your case. We gather all necessary records, contact witnesses, and get statements. We hire experts to help us explain what happened. We keep our clients informed of our investigation throughout our representation.

4. Evaluate

We believe in being candid with our clients about their situations. After we are finished with our investigation, we will answer your questions about the strengths and weaknesses in your case. We will discuss potential outcomes and tell you how much we think a case is worth. You will have the opportunity to have all your questions answered.

5. Resolve If Possible

Many of our cases resolve without filing a lawsuit. We make all attempts to do this when possible. We tell your story to the insurance company and promptly relay any and all offers to you. We will discuss all options of alternative dispute resolution with you.

6. Litigate If Necessary

Sometimes insurance companies don't do what they should. We will not be pushed around. We will file suit if need be and we will hold the defendant accountable so that you are fairly and fully compensated for your harms and losses.

7. Trial

Most of our cases settle before trial. Ironically, this happens because we are willing and able to capably try your case before a jury or a judge. Some firms are just settlers. We're not. We are a trial firm. Every step in our process builds to trial. Insurance companies have no incentive to offer full and fair compensation when they know a lawyer or a law firm is just going to settle. We pride ourselves on trying cases, and insurance companies know this.

This is our proven process. It works.

Fee Agreements

Fortunately many Connecticut injury firms operate on contingency fee agreements, meaning there's no money up front. We only get paid when we recover money for you. This keeps the doors of the courthouse open to the injured. There are two types of contingency fee agreements in Connecticut personal injury cases: 1. a statutory agreement; 2. a statutory waiver agreement.

Fee Agreements in Connecticut Personal Injury Cases Must Be in Writing and Signed

A lawyer in Connecticut cannot receive a fee in a personal injury case if the agreement is not in writing and signed by the client. You should never feel pressured to sign a fee agreement with an attorney. You have the right to read it over and ask questions.

The Statutory Fee Agreement

The language below is taken right out of our firm's standard statutory fee agreement (we call them client agreements). This agreement is set by Connecticut General Statute 52-251c.

Agreement. This is an agreement between the attorney and the client. The client hires the attorney to represent the client with respect to (a)_____ that occurred on _____.

Expenses. The client will pay for all expenses. The client will reimburse the attorney for all expenses advanced by the attorney. "Expenses" include court fees, investigation expenses, expert fees and all other necessary costs. The expenses are in addition to the legal fees.

Legal Fees. The "gross recovery" includes all money that is collected (recovered) from others arising from the matter(s) described in Section III. The legal fees shall be based upon the gross recovery of any award, verdict or settlement arising from the matter(s) as follows:

Thirty-Three (33%) percent of the gross recovery. It is also understood that the following fees are in effect for all sums recovered, by settlement or verdict, in excess of $300,000.00:

Twenty-Dfive (25%) percent of any award or settlement in excess of Three Hundred Thousand ($300,000.00) up to Six Hundred Thousand ($600,000.00) Dollars;

Twenty (20%) percent of the next Three Hundred Thousand ($300,000.00) Dollars;

Fifteen (15%) percent of the next Three Hundred Thousand ($300,000.00) Dollars; and

Ten (10%) percent of any amount which exceeds One Million Two Hundred Thousand ($1,200,000.00) Dollars.

The Statutory Waiver Agreement

In complicated cases, an attorney may ask for a statutory waiver agreement. The statutory waiver agreement waives the limitations set forth by the statutory agreement and will entitle the attorney or law firm up to a fee of 33% of gross amount recovered.

When Does a Statutory Waiver Agreement Apply?

The statute makes it clear that it should only apply to complex claims:

"Notwithstanding the provisions of subsection (b) of this section, a claimant may waive the percentage limitations of said subsection if the claim or civil action is so substantially complex, unique or different from other wrongful death, personal injury or property damage claims or civil actions as to warrant a deviation from such percentage limitations. Factors that may indicate that a claim or civil action is substantially complex, unique or different from other wrongful death, personal injury or property damage claims or civil actions include, but are not limited to, if the claim or civil action (1) involves complex factual medical or legal issues, (2) involves serious permanent personal injury or death,

(3) is likely to require extensive investigation and discovery proceedings, including multiple depositions, or (4) requires independent expert witness testimony. For the purposes of this subsection, "independent expert witness testimony" means testimony, whether at trial or in a deposition, from an expert who has not participated in the care of the claimant and has not participated in any official investigation of the incident involved."

What Are the Requirements For a Statutory Waiver Agreement?

There are very specific steps that an attorney must do to obtain a statutory waiver agreement from a client. They are spelled out by statute:

"(d) Prior to a claimant entering into a contingency fee agreement that provides for a fee that exceeds the percentage limitations of subsection (b) of this section, the attorney shall (1) explain the percentage limitations of subsection (b) of this section to the claimant and the reasons the attorney is unable to abide by those limitations; (2) advise the claimant of the claimant's right to seek representation by another attorney willing to abide by the percentage limitations of subsection (b) of this section; and (3) allow the claimant a sufficient period of time to review the proposed contingency fee agreement and, if the claimant wishes, seek representation by another attorney prior to entering into such agreement.

(e) No waiver of the percentage limitations of subsection (b) of this section shall be valid unless the contingency fee agreement (1) is in writing, (2) sets forth in full the fee schedule of subsection (b) of this section, (3) contains a conspicuous statement, printed in boldface type at least twelve points in size, in substantially the following form: "I UNDERSTAND THAT THE FEE SCHEDULE SET FORTH IN SECTION 52-251c OF THE CONNECTICUT GENERAL STATUTES LIMITS THE AMOUNT OF ATTORNEY'S FEES PAYABLE BY A CLAIMANT AND THAT THE STATUTE WAS INTENDED TO INCREASE THE PORTION OF THE JUDGMENT OR SETTLEMENT THAT WAS ACTUALLY RECEIVED BY A CLAIMANT. NOTWITHSTANDING THAT THE LEGISLATIVE INTENT IN ENACTING THAT FEE SCHEDULE WAS TO CONFER A BENEFIT ON A CLAIMANT LIKE MYSELF, I KNOWINGLY AND VOLUNTARILY WAIVE THAT FEE SCHEDULE IN THIS CLAIM OR CIVIL ACTION.", and (4) is signed and acknowledged by the claimant before a notary public or other person authorized to take acknowledgments."

What Are the Differences Between a Statutory Fee Agreement and a Statutory Waiver Agreement?

Basically, in a complicated case, a statutory waiver agreement will result in a larger fee to the lawyer or law firm. This may be necessary for a firm to economically justify the expense and risk of the litigation.

An attorney cannot seek costs from a client if no recovery is made in a statutory waiver case. (I use the terms "costs" and "expenses" interchangeably; they have the same meaning.) The attorney is responsible for costs in the event of no recovery, not the client. In a statutory fee agreement, it is the client who is responsible for costs in the event of no recovery.

Different firms have different policies on this. It is our belief that the language concerning seeking costs from the client is required by law to be included in a fee agreement, however it is our decision whether or not to actually pursue a client. We don't pursue our clients for costs in the event of no recovery.

Common Expenses in Personal Injury Cases

A lawyer's goal must be to maximize the net recovery (the amount a client gets after expenses and fees). The discussion of expenses needs to happen from the first meeting and continue throughout the representation so aren't any surprises.

Some firms use private investigators to conduct an intake. An intake is an interview to gather basic facts about a case, such as the client's name and address and what happened to cause the client's injury. If an investigator conducts an intake, the client starts the case a $1000 or so in the hole because of the investigator fee. Other firms, like ours, do our own intakes, so there's no cost to the client. Some firms consider postage, copies, mileage, and legal research expenses. We include those costs in our fee. And if we are going to incur travel expenses, we discuss them with the client in advance.

Expenses increase in an injury case over time. At the beginning, the expenses are generally low, but closer to trial, they get higher.

Here are some common expenses in personal injury cases:

Medical Records

Medical providers do not turn over your medical records for free, and many try to charge more for medical records than is currently allowed by law. This is an ongoing battle between Connecticut personal injury firms and providers. By law, electronic records must be inexpensive for patients to obtain, and as of this writing, $6.50 plus postage (if any) has been determined to be a reasonable charge. However, many providers illegally charge $.65 a page—a permissible fee for paper records— for electronic records. We use the following language in our requests to providers in order to educate them about their fees:

"Federal Law 42 USC § 17935 Part (e) of the HITECH statute modifies the HIPAA regulations to limit charges for medical records to cost-based fees for providing records to a patient or "any entity or person designated by the individual, provided that any such choice is clear, conspicuous, and specific; . . ." This statute, which was adopted in 2009, makes the 2007 9th Circuit decision in Webb v. Smart Document Solutions, 499 F.3d, 1078 (2007) moot when a patient requests his or her electronic medical records. Our clients have requested that all electronic records be produced in a .pdf file format on compact disc (CD) for the cost of labor and of a CD. Page charges for a digital file that can be copied to a single CD are not reasonable cost-based fees. The HITECH Act directs that a patient shall have the right to obtain ELECTRONIC RECORDS for a REASONABLE COST-BASED FEE. This has been interpreted to mean $6.50 for a CD-ROM containing records, plus postage."

This is only an excerpt of our letter, which is rather lengthy and dry for the purposes of this discussion. My point is: You should insist that your attorney request electronic records in accordance with the HITECH Act. Medical records can be very expensive to obtain, and that cost will eat into your recovery.

You should also know that the language above isn't magical. Even when we send our long, boring letter explaining the law, many providers won't pay attention and will send an invoice for an illegal charge. We push back as a rule, challenging non-compliant invoices and making complaints to the appropriate HIPAA compliance officers, but this can be a time-consuming process. Sometimes it may be necessary to pay an invoice in order to move your case forward.

Police Reports

Police reports are relatively inexpensive to obtain in Connecticut. The cost generally ranges from $10 to $20.

Investigator

In some cases it is necessary to have an investigator obtain evidence. In order to make the evidence admissible in the event of a trial this person should not be either the attorney working the case or the injured party. An investigator will commonly get sworn witness statements and take pictures of the place where the accident happened . The cost of an investigator is usually between $300 to $750 depending on the scope of the investigation.

Cost of Serving and Filing a Connecticut Personal Injury Lawsuit

At the time of this writing in 2018, the cost to file a lawsuit in Connecticut is $360. Given the current state of Connecticut's budget, it is likely this cost will rise in the future. But as of now, the cost of getting your case on the docket is $360. Papers in Connecticut must be served by a state marshal. The cost of serving papers by a marshal can range from as little as about $100 to as high as about $1000 depending on the number of parties involved and the distance a marshal has to travel.

Jury Claim Fee

Defendants often pay the jury claim fee. The cost of a jury claim in Connecticut is $440. However, sometimes a defendant chooses not to pay a jury claim fee. In that case, a plaintiff must decide whether or not to do so. A case must be claimed to a jury within 10 days of all issues being joined. Otherwise the case will be tried to a judge.

Depositions

It may be necessary to conduct depositions in a case. A deposition is sworn, out-of-court testimony that is normally transcribed or videotaped for use in court. Depositions allow your attorney to find out what happened and have witnesses and defendants commit to statements. They can be a very important tool in discovery. Depositions require court reporters and transcripts. Depending on the length of the deposition, they can run from about $350 to $1500 each.

Experts

Experts are where cases can get really expensive. A case may need experts on liability, medicine, and/or damages. Doctors charge a lot for their testimony. We were recently quoted a rate by a doctor of $2000 an hour. Expert costs vary from field to field so it is impossible to give a range here. But this is another possible expense you must discuss with your attorney.

Takeaways

Attorneys and clients need to have an ongoing discussion of costs on a file. They can really impact the settlement value of a case. For example, an offer of $10,000 pre-suit may net the same money to the client as an offer of $15,000 right before trial.

Our case-management system allows us to share our expenses with our clients in real time. Clients can always see what is being spent on their cases, so there are no unpleasant surprises. We believe knowledge is power.

What to Bring to Your First Attorney Meeting

After you set up a first meeting with an attorney, you will probably have a lot of questions. One question we're asked all the time is, "What documents should I bring to our first meeting?" This post will cover the basics. Don't worry if you don't have all these things. We can have you sign authorizations that will allow us to get them for you. Every personal injury case is different, and each case may require different documents. These eight things are generally good documents to provide to your attorney as soon as possible if you have them.

Driver's License

This is for simple identification purposes. A driver's license tells us the correct spelling of your name, your current address, and your date of birth—all of which we need to have on file.

Health Insurance Card

We work with injured people, so we deal with insurance companies a lot. We need your health insurance information in order to have a full understanding of your coverage and recovery.

Medicare ID

We are required to report claims to Medicare, so if Medicare is covering the medical costs for your injury, we'll need to know this.

Auto Insurance Policy

If you've been in a car accident, we'll need to have your auto insurance policy information on file. Why? We may have to pursue an underinsured motorist claim, or you may have other benefits that we can help you to obtain. You may have medical payment insurance (medpay) benefits.

A Recent Tax Return

If you're missing work because of an injury, a recent tax return tells us who your employer is and what your earnings are. Lost wages are important as we negotiate a settlement or prepare for trial. If your case gets put into suit and there is a lost wage claim, the defense attorney will be entitled to three years of tax returns.

Accident Photos

If you have 'em, we need 'em. Accident photos are critical documents as we negotiate a settlement or prepare for litigation. More immediately, they help us understand what happened to you.

Police Report or Accident Summary

If you were just in a car accident and the police were called to the scene, the reporting officer probably gave you a slip of paper. This is an accident summary. We use this document to order a police report and to identify the person or persons who struck your vehicle. The accident summary will contain their insurance policy information, which we will use to send a letter of representation to their insurance company.

Medical Documents

If you happen to have bills or medical records, please bring them. If not, don't sweat it. We ask all our clients to sign a release so that we can order their complete medical records pertaining to their injury.

That about covers it. If we need anything extra from our clients, we discuss it at our meeting. But bringing these documents gives us what we need to hit the ground running. These are the documents in personal injury cases that will help your lawyer prosecute your case.

Medical Bills

Who pays co-pays?

I just selected my health insurance plan for the coming year. The co-pays are high. If I—or a member of my family—were in a car accident, the co-pays could be budget busting. As an attorney, it's no surprise that I'm often asked about co-pays. With most folks' budgets stretched thin, co-pays can present a real problem. Unfortunately, you will need to pay your co-pays during your treatment.

Why should I have to pay co-pays? The car accident was not my fault.

Under Connecticut law, it is the injured victim's obligation to pay medical bills, including co-pays. It doesn't matter who caused the wreck. If the other driver is at fault, your remedy is to seek reimbursement from the person who hit you.

Why does the at-fault driver's insurance company not pay my co-pays?

Car insurance companies will not pay "as you go" for medical treatment. Insurance adjusters will only reimburse for medical treatment after all treatment has ended. Unfortunately for those without health insurance or the ability to pay, this frequently means they will have to forego necessary medical treatment or borrow money to pay for it.

Will my doctor treat me if promise to pay after my settlement?

Some healthcare providers will not provide treatment under a promise to pay later. Others will agree to accept a letter of protection from an attorney. A letter of protection is a contract from you and your lawyer agreeing to pay the doctor for medical fees out of any settlement or verdict.

Will my auto insurance pay my medical bills?

Your car insurance company is not responsible for paying for medical bills stemming from a car accident. Some Connecticut insurance policies do have "medical payments" coverage, or medpay. This is additional insurance that must be purchased prior to your accident. Medpay will provide money for things like bills and co-pays.

What can I do about co-pays?

The stress of these co-pays is often overwhelming for an injured person. Many folks choose not to get the treatment they need because they can't pay the co-pays. That's not right.

The good news is that you have options. We keep a list of medical providers who will take folks on a letter of protection. A letter of protection means your co-pays will be paid to the provider out of any settlement or verdict. We can explore the option of a loan against a potential settlement from a third party lender.

It is important to keep the copay bills and send them to your lawyer. That way you can be assured they are paid in any settlement.

Dealing with Insurance Companies

Why is it taking so long to settle my claim? Why won't the insurance company believe my doctors? Why do I have to go through a medical exam? Why is my deposition taking so long? Why do they keep trying to continue court? Why are they saying I'm at fault when I'm not? A dog didn't cause the wreck. That's not true! I was there. I remember.

Injured folks everywhere ask these kinds of questions.

We know why. We've been there.

Insurance companies make massive profits by: delaying, denying, and defending. Claims centers are now profit centers.

"An insurance company can make a lot of money on the small claims," said Jay Feinman, a professor at Rutgers University School of Law, "because if you save a few dollars on a huge number of claims, it's worth more than saving a lot of dollars on a very small number of claims."

Do I have to talk to their insurance company? That's a common question I'm asked.

My introduction to personal injury law came as a client. I had just graduated from high school. I was driving my girlfriend home when a man T-boned me. He totaled my car and I was hurt.

While I was hurt, the other driver's insurance company kept calling me. They wanted to interview me, to get my side of what happened – as if there were some other side. The guy didn't look where he was going and plowed into the passenger side of my car. The cops cited the other guy for failing to yield the right of way.

I was in some serious pain and yet the adjuster kept calling me.

The emergency room gave me some muscle relaxers. I was out of it and in no place to give a statement to anyone.

That's when my parents called an attorney. It all felt so overwhelming. There were rental cars, doctor's appointments, missed work, and property settlement negotiations.

I'll never forget that first meeting in the lawyer's office.

He said, "Ryan, their insurance company is not your friend. They are out for themselves. They'll record your call. They'll ask, "How are you?" And if you respond politely and say, "I'm doing all right," they'll use it against you. They'll say you weren't that hurt because you said you were all right."

That was twenty years ago. That advice is still true to this day. Insurance companies are no friend to the injured. No matter how nice the representatives may seem, they're out for one thing – to make money on your injury.

After you're in a car wreck, you may find yourself asking the question that I was asking myself in the summer of 1997. "Do I have to talk to their insurance company?"

The answer is no. At least, not before speaking with an attorney who has your interests at heart.

Everything you say can and will be used against you.

Before you talk to their insurance company, you should talk to a personal injury lawyer who has experience talking to insurance companies.

I've seen them twist words. I've been there. And I was fortunate to have great counsel to help me be made as whole as possible.

Insurance Company Tactic #1: Offering You Money to Go Away.

You were in a car accident. The other person's insurance company claims they have "accepted responsibility" and they want you to sign releases. They want you to sign a release giving them access to your medical records and another one saying that

you won't sue. You're not a lawsuit-happy person–
you just want what is fair. The insurance company
tells you that if you hire a lawyer you will get less
money because the lawyer will take a fee. But you
wonder whether you should speak with a lawyer
anyway.

The insurance company is deploying advanced
psychological tactics to get you to accept their offer.
One of the tactics is loss aversion: in most people's
minds, it's better to not lose $5 than to find $5.

The reason the insurance company is deploying
these tactics is in hopes of saving a buck. If the car
accident claim is objectively worth 20k and they can
get a release for 2k – they look at it as making 18k
on your car accident claim.

Bottom line: Have your case evaluated by a
personal injury lawyer.

Tell your lawyer about the offer. An honest
lawyer will give you a straight evaluation if possible,
and usually it is easy. Usually the reason the
insurance company has offered money at all is
because they know the claim is worth many times
what they are offering.

I can't speak for other lawyers, but I will not
accept a case where I can't put my client in a better
position. If the insurance company has offered a

potential client $3,000, then I have to be sure I can get that potential client something more. Otherwise, if the client hires me and I take a third of that $3,000, the client will only receive $2,000 and I will have made the client worse off. That's not fair.

Insist on a free case evaluation. Insist that your lawyer not take the case if they can't help you. Get it in writing in your fee agreement.

Whatever insurance company is representing the person who injured you is doing whatever they can to prevent you from recovering for the harms and losses that you've suffered. Make no mistake about it – they're out to get you.

Insurance Company Tactic #2: Hiring a Private Investigator to Follow You.

One of their "go to" tactics is to hire a private investigator to stalk you. They'll pay some goon squad to video tape you grocery shopping. The primary reason insurance companies do this is to intimidate someone their insured has injured into settling their claim for less than fair value. Frankly, it's bullshit.

At Connecticut Trial Firm, we arm our clients against the goon squad. Here are some simple tips:

1. Talk with your neighbors. Ask them to report any unusual vehicles in your neighborhood. Ask

them to say something (that is, call the police) if they see something.

2. If you think you are being watched, call the police. If at all possible, get the vehicle's license plates.

3. When it's safe to do so, turn your cell phone's video camera on and film the goons.

4. Immediately notify your lawyer that you are being followed.

Understand that they're doing this to scare you. Being stalked is no joke. Consider going to counseling to address these fears.

Don't let them intimidate you. That's all they want. They want you to lose sleep thinking there's someone in the bushes at your family picnic. That's because insurance companies aren't above putting a goon in those very bushes.

Dirty insurance company tactics are so prevalent in Connecticut that we have strategies to deal with them. For example, with some insurers we file suit immediately because know they won't pay reasonable value until the time of trial. No need to wait a year to file suit – that wait year is a wasted year. Best to push the case forward.

Healing Yourself

A book on a personal injury law practice is incomplete without a chapter on healing. As mentioned earlier, part of my job as an attorney is to make you whole under the law, but you're never going to feel "whole" until you heal physically and emotionally from your injury. For this reason, I always regard my clients as complete human beings and not simply people in need of legal services. It's important to me that you treat your injuries appropriately, whether that treatment includes talking to a therapist or attending sessions with a chiropractor.

If you are injured, put yourself first.

I know when I was in a car wreck, the first thing I did was tell the EMTs I was fine. I didn't need an ambulance. Hours later I was in the ER in severe pain–pain that lasted for days.

Clients often ask, "What do I do?" Our answer is that you do everything you can to get better.

Many folks aren't comfortable putting themselves first. Right now you may feel powerless. You have been wronged. But the wheels of justice spin slowly.

The best thing you can do is take care of yourself. Follow your doctor's orders, keep your medical appointments, and do your home exercises. Rest if you need rest.

Be honest with your doctor about your progress. If you are in pain, tell them. If something new hurts, tell them. Tell your treating physician what you were like before. For example, "I never felt this before the car accident." This will help your doctors understand the impact the accident has had on you. Let others help you.

Most importantly, take care of yourself. This is the first step in taking back your life.

Sometimes the physical pain of an injury is so great that a person forgets the loss he suffered that day was so much more than the damage to his body. My clients often suffer emotionally, too. You may feel isolated, which means feeling alone but also means feeling like someone other than yourself. You always used to get up and go to CrossFit, but getting back together with your friends for an honest workout feels a long way off. Now it's all about getting through the next twenty-four hours. Forget burpees – getting out of bed is difficult enough.

Isolation hurts – badly. You message your friends on Facebook, but it's not the same. You see pictures of their workouts. But you're not in those pictures. You think about unfollowing your friends on Facebook. It all feels so strange. So awful.

Signs You Are Feeling Isolated After a Personal Injury

1. *Your routine is off.* You used to get up at 4:30 every morning to go work out. And now you can't. Now you sleep. Your whole day feels different.

2. *Your friends treat you differently.* They try not to, but they do. They support you, but they used to say things after you missed a day like, "You're gonna kill this workout because you're so well-rested." Now they are just wishing you well.

3. *Social media makes you feel worse.* You log in to Facebook and see others engaging in activities you can no longer participate in. And while you're happy for them, you feel sad because it is a cold reminder of who you used to be.

4. *You are not sleeping well.* You haven't just lost the use of part of your body. You have lost the use of part of yourself. You lie awake at night wondering if you'll ever get back. And if you do, if it will ever be the same.

5. *You are alone more of the time.* You day used to be gym, then work, then back home. Now

A Practical Guide To Connecticut Personal Injury Law

you are just watching TV all day. And daytime television is depressing as hell.

6. You miss your old self. You would give anything for the injury not to have happened. Anything to get back to your normal life.

How to Regain Control

You've been through a traumatic experience. You continue to be traumatized. What's happening now is not sustainable. You know this.

It's time to change things. It's time to regain control.

Here's what you need to do:

1. Acknowledge Your Situation

Denial isn't acceptable. The first step toward exiting survival mode is acknowledging that it's happening. Tell yourself: This is not normal. This is not sustainable.

If you are feeling isolated, it is important to recognize this. To feel it. To acknowledge it. And to do nothing more.

The road to recovery may be a long one, and you may have to acknowledge that some things will never be the same.

2. Ask for Help

We're proud of our strengths and our self-sufficiency. We're embarrassed when things break down. You had no problem getting advice on training and nutrition at the gym. Now is the time to seek mental health coaching. It can make all the difference.

Ask for help. If your employer offers an employee assistance program that offers free counseling, take it if you need it. Do not suffer alone.

3. Make New Plans

You had a life before your injury. You had plans – plans that likely didn't involve getting injured.

The only way to move forward is to think long-term and execute deliberately. You've got to see the future, determine what you need to build it, and then commit to making it happen.

Find something new that interests you. Something that excites you. And seek some new community that can help support you.

4. Tell Your Friends You Are Feeling Isolated

Folks by and large want to help. Many people are really good at it, but those same people may not be good at recognizing how much someone may be suffering. Don't assume your community understands what you are going through. They likely do not. Tell them. Give them the opportunity to connect with you.

Feeling all alone is one of the worst feelings anyone can experience. Let someone you trust know you're feeling this way.

5. Know That This Too Shall Pass

Suffering in silence won't fix the problem.

Recognizing and then acknowledging your feelings and asking for help can improve your situation.

Remember this feeling too shall pass. You will have new normals. You will fight to get back to where you were. Your body will heal in some way. It may be different than it was before, but it will be better than it is now.

Recognize that your whole person was hurt that day. Not just your body.

I've been there. I've been there as someone injured in a car wreck. It was scary. It was awful. Almost 20 years later, I clench my jaw thinking about that day. Metallica is playing on the radio. It is sunny, then *bam*. There's this awful noise. A noise

I'll never forget. Then there is confusion. And that's just the immediate aftermath. Later there is anxiety. There is anger. There is fear of what could have been. I get it.

I've also been there with my clients. At funerals. At hospitals. In their homes. In my office. I very much feel their pain.

There is sadness. There is loss.

I was listening to a podcast and the topic was happiness.

Unsurprisingly, instability of affairs makes people unhappy. If you find yourself in the hospital, the stability of your world has been upended. Am I going to get better? Will I walk again? Who is going to take care of my pet? When can I go back to work?

Stability leads to happiness.

If you have been injured, seek stability wherever you can find it. Maybe you find it in a new routine, something as simple as starting your day with your favorite breakfast food. Maybe you find stability in taking a short walk. Maybe you find it in the companionship of others. Anything that is stable will help you heal – even binge-watching a series on Netflix.

For me, the routine of exercises from physical therapy helped me feel better. It was a stable routine.

I understand that it isn't your leg that is injured. The injury is to your whole person.

As a lawyer, I can provide you with some stability. I can take problems off your plate. I can be there for you. This is why I do the work I do.

Damages

One of the questions we're often asked is, "How much is my case worth?" In order to answer, we have to look at what the law can award for damages. In Connecticut, plaintiffs can be compensated for both "economic" and "non-economic" damages. What is the difference?

"Economic damages" are compensation for pecuniary losses including – but not limited to – medical care, rehabilitative services, custodial care, and loss of earnings or earning capacity. "Non-economic damages" are for all nonpecuniary losses, including loss of enjoyment of life, physical pain and suffering, and mental and emotional suffering.

We're often asked, "How do I calculate pain and suffering?" The answer is perhaps unsatisfactory to folks who like certainty. There is no formula to enable a jury to arrive at an award for pain and suffering damages. Our Supreme Court, in *Jerz v. Humphrey*, 160 Conn. 219 (1971), held that the determination of damages rests within the discretion of the trier of fact. A trier of fact is a jury in a jury trial or a judge in a bench trial.

Appellate courts routinely uphold generous awards of pain and suffering damages. Jury verdicts on pain and suffering are only overturned for things like corruption, prejudice, or partiality.

Yes, it's uncertain, but it makes sense. The role of the jury is very important. Every case is different. It is the jury who must balance the scales of justice and vote on a verdict that reflects the harms and losses of someone who has suffered an injury.

We carefully evaluate every case we take through confidential methods to arrive at an amount of money for pain and suffering that is just and reasonable. The jury is the conscience of the community. The founding fathers got this right. We ultimately calculate damages for pain and suffering by asking the community.

Damages in Car Accident Cases

In car collisions there are three types of damage. The first is the damage to the people in the car, the second is the damage to the car itself, and the third is the damage to the property inside of the car.

In many instances, insurance companies just offer folks money for the damage to the car. If the car is totaled, they have to pay for the value of the car. If the car is damaged, they have to pay to fix the damage.

Insurance companies almost never offer to fix any property that was damaged in the car.

Car Seats

One of the most common items of personal property that gets damaged in car accidents are car seats – and with good reason. The National Highway Transportation Safety Board recommends that child safety seats and boosters be replaced following a moderate or severe crash in order to ensure a continued high level of crash protection for child passengers.

I have young children, and I can tell you that car seats are both important and expensive. There is nothing more important than the safety of our children, but coming up with several hundred dollars to replace car seats you planned on getting years out of is tough for many folks.

The thing is, insurance companies have one goal: to pay you as little as possible for what someone did to you. It doesn't matter how nice their claims rep is. They are trying to screw you. They will not tell you what your rights are, and you have the right to be made whole.

The law of Pottery Barn is the law of the land. *If you break it, you own it.*

If your car seats are broken in a wreck, you have the right to be compensated for them by the other person's insurance company. Know your rights. Knowledge is power.

And if the insurance company says they'll pay you the diminished value of the car seats, fight back. Don't let them give you that nonsense. Their insured hurt you. Make them own it – all of it. And if you think they are nickel-and-diming you on a car seat, that is only the beginning. Car seats are cheap compared to medical bills.

Diminished Value

So you've been in a car wreck and the shop is doing repairs. Maybe they have even given you a decent rental car. The insurance company for the person who hit you is paying for the repairs. But before the accident, you were thinking about selling your car, and now you're not sure. Who wants to buy a car that has been in a wreck? I mean, someone will, but no one is interested in paying full value. Even when your car is fixed, it's not going to be worth what it was worth last week.

Should the insurance company have to pay for your car's loss of value? The answer is yes.

Connecticut law says that when someone is at fault in an accident, they have an obligation to make the person they hit whole. Not half whole. Not partially whole. But whole-whole. This means they have to pay for your repairs, your rental car, your loss of income, your medical bills, your pain and suffering, and any future medical bills.

If You Are at Fault

In Connecticut, a claim under a person's personal auto insurance policy ("first-party claim") for diminution of value is typically not covered. The policy language specifies that the insurance covers the cost of repairing the vehicle or, if considered a total loss, the actual cash value. It does not specify payment for lost market value. The policy may even include specific language excluding coverage for diminution in value.

If Someone Else Is at Fault

Connecticut holds the negligent person responsible for the diminished value of the vehicle. A person whose vehicle is damaged in an accident may submit a claim for diminution of value against the negligent driver's auto insurance policy. The policy's property damage liability coverage pays for this. The measure of damages recoverable is the vehicle's reasonable market value before the accident, minus its reasonable market value after the accident, plus interest from the date of loss.

What to Do

The fact that the insurance company has to pay for the loss of your car is bedrock Connecticut law (*Littlejohn v. Elionsky*, 130 Conn. 541, 36 A.2d 52 (1944)). Insurance companies often try and tell people the law does not cover loss of value. Or they lie through omission by telling them nothing at all. (Remember: insurance companies are not your friend.) These kinds of claims are called diminished-value claims.

I'm not a property damage lawyer. I don't take any fee on property damage claims from car wrecks. I'm an injury lawyer who understands that often one of the first problems my clients face is getting their car fixed after a wreck. I know. I've been there. The last thing you want to deal with as you're trying to heal is an insurance company out to pay you as little as they possibly can. If they treat your property value claim unfairly, you can imagine how they're going to treat your injury claim.

What about rental cars?

If someone else damages your property, you are entitled to compensation for loss of use of that property – including a rental vehicle. You are entitled to a comparable rental vehicle for a reasonable period of time necessary to settle your claim or repair your vehicle. A reasonable period of time for depends on the amount of time needed to repair the vehicle.

You may also have rental coverage under your own policy. Check with your insurance company. This may provide additional benefits to you. I never take a fee for property damage, including rental cars.

They're Suing for What?

This morning while making breakfast, I had a local news station on. Somewhere between making the coffee and my English muffin, I heard a newscaster say, "So-and-so is suing so-and-so for fifteen thousand dollars." I thought to myself, "Probably not."

I hear this several times a year on the news, so I figure I'll use this space to clear things up. In some states, I've seen pleadings that read that the plaintiff demands $1,456,103.27 or some other crazy number. But in Connecticut state courts, that's not how it works. The plaintiff is only required to attach a jurisdictional pleading that reads something like this: "The Plaintiff seeks money damages which are within the jurisdiction of the court and the amount of which exclusive of interest and costs is in excess of Fifteen Thousand ($15,000.00) Dollars."

This language has nothing to do with what the plaintiff is actually seeking in the case. In Connecticut, cases are categorized based on the size of the claim. Cases where the plaintiff is seeking under five thousand dollars will go to the small claims court, while claims between five and fifteen thousand dollars will be handled by a different docket. When we use this language in our pleadings, we are telling the court that this case needs to be handled as a case worth in excess of fifteen thousand dollars. In fact, such language is applicable to cases where the plaintiff is seeking hundreds of thousands or even millions of dollars in damages.

Statutes of Limitation

When you get hurt – whether you are in a car accident or you are a victim of malpractice – it is a confusing time. What are your rights? Should you get a lawyer? What is fair? Those are questions that run through many people's heads.

If you've been injured in Connecticut, it's important to be aware of the various statutes of limitation.

A statute of limitation is simply the statutory deadline for filing a lawsuit. After this deadline passes, it's too late to bring a case against the person who caused your injury.

We want your focus to be on healing, first and foremost. But part of ensuring that you are healed may mean recovering money for future medical expenses. This is why it's important to talk to a personal injury attorney soon after you've been hurt. You don't want to miss a crucial deadline.

Here are the basic types of personal injury cases in Connecticut and the deadlines for filing a lawsuit:

Statutes of Limitation for negligence or recklessness / medical malpractice: two years from when an injury is "sustained or discovered," not to

exceed three years from the date of the act. Conn. Gen. Stat. Sec. 52-584.

Injuries aren't always obvious. In a medical malpractice context, you may be injured but not discover the cause until some time has passed. This statute recognizes that situation somewhat by allowing suit to be filed up to three years from the date of the negligent or reckless act. **However, this is not a three-year statute of limitation!** Once you learn the cause of your injury, you have two years to file suit **at the very most**. If you discover you were injured by an act that occurred two years and six months ago, you only have six months, and **only** if you couldn't have reasonably discovered your injury sooner.

I can't stress enough that it is very important to speak with an attorney immediately after discovering an injury.

Statute of Limitation for wrongful death: two years from death, not to exceed five years from the date of the act. Conn. Gen. Stat. Sec. 52-555.

This one comes with a big exception for criminal acts like murder. If someone is found legally responsible for causing a death and has been convicted or found not guilty by reason of a mental disease or defect, then the statute of limitation does not apply.

Statute of Limitation for intentional acts, legal malpractice, and other torts: three years. Conn. Gen. Stat. Sec. 52-577.

As I learned in law school, a "tort" is not a delicious dessert. Torts include conduct like trespass and fraud.

Statute of Limitations for product liability: three years, generally speaking. Conn. Gen. Stat. Sec. 52-577a.

There are exceptions to the rule, but they are too complicated for the purposes of this post. If you think you have a claim, definitely talk to an attorney about it.

Statute of Limitations for uninsured/underinsured motorist claims: three years, generally speaking. Conn. Gen. Stat. Sec. 38a-336(g)(1)

Again, there are exceptions to the rule and ways to toll (suspend) the statute of limitations. An attorney can evaluate how these laws apply to your case.

Notice Requirements

Time is not your friend if you have a personal injury claim. Statutes of limitation are important because these are your deadlines for filing a lawsuit. However, sometimes you must provide notice of a potential claim long before a lawsuit is filed. This is called a "notice requirement." Miss a notice requirement, and the case is finished. If a lawyer fails to give notice, then malpractice may result.

In short, it is critical that notice be given properly and timely. It's so important that I mention notice requirements several times in this book in different contexts to make it abundantly clear.

Here are some general notice requirements that arise in the personal injury context:

Claims against the State:

One year from when a claim is "sustained or discovered," not to exceed three years. Claims must be filed with the Claims Commissioner. (Conn. Gen. Stat. Sec. 4-148)

Defective highway claims:

Trip and fall on a sidewalk in Connecticut? You have a mere **ninety days** to provide notice to the proper state or municipal authority.

This is an enormous trap for the unwary – plaintiffs and lawyers alike. Notice of state claims must be filed with the Commissioner of Transportation (Conn. Gen. Stat. Sec. 13a-144). You must file a notice of a claim against a municipality with the appropriate authority, which varies from town to town. (Conn. Gen. Stat. Sec. 13a-149). Assuming the notice requirements are met, you have two years from the date of injury to file suit.

Dram shop actions:

If you want to bring an action against a bar in Connecticut, you've got to do so quickly. You've got **120 days** from the date of injury, or **180 days** from the date of death or incapacity, to provide notice of your claim. The statute specifies the information that must be included in this letter, so be sure to read it closely. Conn. Gen. Stat. Sec. 30-102.

Once you send that dram shop letter, it's time to move quickly on the lawsuit. You've only got one year.

Notice of housing authority claims:

If you've been injured on property owned or controlled by a housing authority, you must give notice of a claim within six months of the injury before filing suit. A lawsuit must be filed within two years. Conn. Gen. Stat. Sec. 8-67.

Municipal employee negligence claims:

When bringing a claim against a municipal employee, you must provide notice to the municipality within six months. A lawsuit must be filed within two years. Conn. Gen. Stat. Sec. 7-465.

Claims against volunteer firefighters, volunteer ambulance members, and volunteer fire police officers:

You must file notice of a claim with the town **and** with the volunteer firefighter, volunteer ambulance member, or volunteer fire police officer not later than six months after the date of injury. Then you have to wait at least thirty days before filing a lawsuit. Any such lawsuit must be filed within one year. Conn. Gen. Stat. Sec. 7-308.

It is important if you have been injured to immediately contact a personal injury attorney to protect your claim. Failing to file notice or proper notice can result in no recovery. Attorneys who fail to comply with these statutes can be subject to legal malpractice.

I've been there, running along a sidewalk on a nice fall morning. I'm enjoying the crisp weather, looking at what is ahead of me – and suddenly I'm on the ground. Fortunately, aside from a scrape, I'm okay. I look back to see what caused my fall and I notice the sidewalk is uneven. I'm lucky. I don't need to make a claim. Not everyone is so lucky. Falls on sidewalks can result in serious injuries.

In Connecticut, one of the harshest statutes we have is the sidewalk notice statute. Many folks are injured on Connecticut's sidewalks – often because towns fail to maintain or inspect them. If you were injured on a sidewalk, then you need to seek a personal injury attorney as soon as possible. Connecticut allows a person who was injured by means of a defective sidewalk to recover damages from the party obligated to keep it in good repair. However, before claiming that a person was injured because of a defective sidewalk, the plaintiff must provide the required statutory notice of injury.

No notice, no case. It's that simple and that harsh.

The law requires that an action can only be brought to recover damages caused by a defective sidewalk if the plaintiff provides written notice of the injury with a general description of the injury, the cause, the time, and the place of its occurrence. This notice must be given within ninety days of the injury to a selectman or clerk of the town, city, or borough bound to keep the sidewalk in repair.

Your lawyer should immediately investigate the sidewalk. You should accompany your lawyer to the location of the fall. Pictures should be taken. Your lawyer should do a title search to determine ownership of the sidewalk. Your lawyer also needs to examine town ordinances related to sidewalks.

All this has to be done within ninety days of the fall. If it is not, you cannot make any claim for your injuries. But it's worth noting that giving notice doesn't mean you have to pursue a claim. Giving notice simply preserves your right to bring a claim if you and your attorney decide to do so.

Drunk Driving

It happens all too often. You're driving safely down the road, obeying the speed limit. Your seatbelt is on and your eyes are on the road. You are doing everything you're supposed to be doing when suddenly an oncoming car swerves into your lane and hits your vehicle head-on. You later learn that the other driver was drunk. You did everything right, but now you are the one suffering for their poor decision: the inexcusable decision to get behind the wheel while intoxicated.

How Many People Have Been Killed by Drunk Drivers in Connecticut?

Drunk driving ruins lives. According to the Centers for Disease Control and Prevention, drunk driving is a serious problem in Connecticut. Here, over 2% of drivers report driving after drinking too much—a number that is higher than the national average. Nearly forty percent of traffic fatalities in Connecticut involve a driver with a blood alcohol content (BAC) of .08 or higher, which is considered legally alcohol-impaired. One thousand thirty-nine people were killed by drunk drivers in Connecticut between 2003 and 2012. That's 1,039 mothers, fathers, sons, and daughters who never made it home. Many more people are permanently injured.

Drunk driving is far too common in Connecticut.

How can we change these troubling statistics? First and foremost, we can make the choice to drive responsibly. We can offer to serve as a designated driver or refrain from drinking when we know we will be driving home. Aside from this, Connecticut law provides for tough penalties for drunk drivers, but it's often up to juries to enforce those laws – particularly on the civil side.

Drunk driving is per se reckless driving under Connecticut law. Any person who drives recklessly is liable for double or treble damages in a civil action. When a jury in a civil case involving a drunk driver finds that driver liable to an injured party for double or treble damages, this sends a very strong message to the community that drunk driving will not be tolerated in our state. Double or treble damages means double or triple the amount a jury awards a victim of drunk driving. So if a jury decides the driver should pay you $50,000 in damages and also awards punitive damages, the judge can double or triple that $50,000 award. This is a powerful way that we as citizens can change Connecticut for the better.

Our laws only mean something if juries hold wrongdoers accountable. To fail to do so is to reward bad conduct. And we know that bad conduct rewarded is bad conduct repeated. For many victims, it's about a lot more than money.

What can an attorney for victims of drunk drivers do?

If you've been injured in an accident involving a drunk driver, know that we understand how your life can change in an instant through no fault of your own. Victims of drunk drivers need a lawyer who understands. They need a lawyer who will fight for them – fight in both civil and criminal courts.

Injuries caused by an Uber Driver

It's been a long week. The good news? It's finally the weekend, and you've hired a sitter to watch the kids so you and your partner can go out for a nice dinner. You enjoy yourselves (and a bottle of wine) a little too much, so you decide to call an Uber for a ride home. Your driver is very personable and you are happy with your decision. It's the responsible thing to do.

But on the way home, the Uber driver misses a curve on the highway, violently striking the median. You and your partner are taken by ambulance to the hospital.

Now what?

There are five things you need to know if you've been in an accident with an Uber driver in Connecticut.

Laws protect you if you are in an Uber car accident in Connecticut. But you have to make sure you properly preserve your rights or they can be lost forever. The same laws also apply to Lyft.

1. Uber drivers in Connecticut have to follow Connecticut law.

Transportation network companies (Uber, Lyft, etc.) are allowed to operate in Connecticut pursuant to Public Act 17-140. This law requires the companies to register with the Connecticut Commissioner of Transportation each year. If they fail to follow the law, then they will no longer be permitted to operate in the state. If they operate in the state without a valid registration, they can be fined up to $50,000.

2. Uber is required to conduct background checks on their drivers.

Legally, your Uber driver is supposed to have a clean driving record and a clean background check before Uber can hire him or her. This means that any Uber driver who works in Connecticut has undergone a criminal background check that includes submitting fingerprints to the FBI. Once hired, this process is repeated every three years. Among other things, Uber must verify that your driver has not been convicted of driving under the influence of alcohol or drugs within the last seven years.

If you observe anything suspicious about a driver, you should report it to Uber through the policy it is required to post on its website (www.uber.com).

3) Your Uber driver is supposed to be a good driver.

Uber cannot hire any driver who, in the last three years, has (1) committed more than three moving violations in the previous three years or (2) committed one serious traffic violation. Under Conn. Gen. Stat. Sec. 14-1, "serious traffic violation" means:

> a conviction of any of the following offenses: (A) Excessive speeding, involving a single offense in which the speed is fifteen miles per hour or more above the posted speed limit, in violation of section 14-218a or 14-219; (B) reckless driving in violation of section 14-222; (C) following too closely in violation of section 14-240 or 14-240a; (D) improper or erratic lane changes, in violation of section 14-236; (E) using a hand-held mobile telephone or other electronic device or typing, reading or sending text or a text message with or from a mobile telephone or mobile electronic device in violation of subsection (e) of section 14-296aa while operating a commercial motor vehicle; (F)

driving a commercial motor vehicle without a valid commercial driver's license in violation of section 14-36a or 14-44a; (G) failure to carry a commercial driver's license in violation of section 14-44a; (H) failure to have the proper class of license or endorsement, or violation of a license restriction in violation of section 14-44a; or (I) a violation of any provision of chapter 248, by an operator who holds a commercial driver's license or instruction permit that results in the death of another person.

That said, Connecticut does allow Uber drivers to work long hours: up to fourteen consecutive hours, and up to sixteen hours in a twenty-four hour period. That's potentially a lot of driving, and even the best drivers can make mistakes when they're tired. It is worth noting that Uber is required to have policies prohibiting any driver from operating a vehicle when that driver is likely to be impaired by illness or fatigue.

4) Any vehicle used by an Uber driver is required to be in good condition.

Any Uber driver is required to certify to Uber that his or her vehicle is in good working condition. For example, brakes, taillights, and seat belts must work and the tires must be safe. Your Uber vehicle must have four doors, and it must not be designed to transport more than eight people, including the driver.

5) Uber is required to insure its drivers.

Uber is required to insure its drivers when they're working. If a driver is shown on the transportation network as available to give rides, then that driver must be covered by a $50,000 per person bodily injury policy ($100,000 per accident). If the Uber driver is "engaged in the provision of a prearranged ride," then that insurance policy increases to one million dollars per accident.

It's important to note that a driver's personal car insurance policy may not be available when that driver is driving for Uber. It's likely that anyone injured by a working Uber driver will not be able to pursue the driver's personal insurance policy.

Wrongful Death

The first steps in a Connecticut wrongful death claim are important steps.

I've been there with clients. I've been at the homes of grieving families. Folks who thought their loved one was coming home. Folks who got that call or who answered a knock to find a police officer at their door. It's devastating, and it is the most sacred honor in my career to help a family through this time. To listen, to answer the calls, to work with the police and the media, and to make sure the legal system starts working for them. That's the job of a wrongful death lawyer.

What Is a Wrongful Death Claim?

"Wrongful death" claims can arise from a number of different kinds of events, including: car accidents, assaults, medical malpractice, unsafe premises, construction or workplace accidents, unsafe roads or sidewalks, dog bites, airplane or train crashes, motorcycle crashes, truck crashes, and negligent security. Basically any wrongful act that results in a death could result in a wrongful death claim. A wrongful death claim is brought under Connecticut General Statute 52-555.

How Long Do I Have to Bring a Wrongful Death Claim?

Generally, all claims for negligence in Connecticut must be brought within two years of the act that caused the death. There are some exceptions to this, though in some cases, notices have to be sent to proper parties within as little as 90 days to preserve a claim. This requires that an attorney be diligent and cover all bases. For example, a defective road notice may have to be given before a police report has been released. Independent of any police investigation, a wrongful death lawyer needs to immediately commence an independent investigation.

What Is the First Step in Bringing s Connecticut Wrongful Death Claim?

First, an estate must be opened in probate court. An administrator or executor of the estate must be appointed. An administrator is a person who handles the estate of a person without a will. An executor is a person who handles the estate of a person who died with a will. The administrator or executor must inform the probate court of the wrongful death claim and begin prosecuting it. This often involves hiring an attorney to handle the action. Failing to properly preserve a wrongful death action can result in the administrator or executor being sued. It's important that the administrator or executor do his or her job properly.

Good wrongful death lawyers are curious historians. In every other kind of case, the person who is injured tells me what happened. This does not happen in a wrongful death cases. The best things a good wrongful death lawyer can do is to get out of the office and into the loved one's family. Go to their kitchen table. Go to their job. Retrace their steps. Watch home movies. Look through the funeral guest book and reach out to folks. There's more to be done, but that's the start.

Damages in Wrongful Death Cases

Few things are as difficult in law as calculating wrongful death damages.

Life is the rarest thing in the universe. There is a lot of rock out there. A lot of dust too. But in the scope of all we know, human life is truly unique and special. It's hard to put a price on it.

Connecticut law compensates plaintiffs in wrongful death cases for both economic and non-economic damages. Non-economic damages in the wrongful death action consist of (1) any pain and suffering experienced before death, (2) the loss of the life itself, and (3) the destruction of the ability to continue life's activities.

What the Jury Can Consider for Wrongful Death Damages

In evaluating the damages for the loss of the life and the destruction of the ability to continue life's activities, the fact finder must consider the details of the decedent's life. The lawyer for decedent's estate must present an overall picture of the decedent's activities to enable the jury to make an informed evaluation of the decedent's inability to carry on life's activities. For example, the fact finder may consider the loss of the ability to marry and have a family or the loss of the ability to pursue a career and become involved in community activities. Hobbies, recreational activities, and the inability to attend important future events may be considered. For example, if the decedent was a lifelong Cubs fan and they win the World Series just after his death – a jury may consider that as a compensable event.

What the Jury Can't Consider for Wrongful Death Damages

The jury can't consider the issues from the standpoint of the estate's beneficiaries. This is a difficult prism in which these cases operate. The tears of a son missing a father aren't to be considered. What a jury considers is the father's loss of spending time with his son. The financial needs of the beneficiaries can't be considered. It doesn't matter if the kids are wealthy or poor, and the remarriage of the decedent's spouse does not affect the damages for the wrongful death.

Wrongful Death Summary

The wrongful death cases I have worked on have been some of the hardest cases of my career. Figuring out how to capture the essence of the person who has been killed requires a lot of time and a lot of empathy. It means going to dark places in order to understand the void the loss has created in the universe. It means going to the person's home, sitting in their chair, going to where they worked, and sharing a meal with the family. It means spending time in their house and looking at the books they loved, trying to get to know who the person was. It is the only way any lawyer can convey the loss of a father, mother, son, or daughter to a jury, judge, or mediator.

Defective Road Claims

Connecticut law provides that a person who was injured by means of a defective road may recover damages from the party bound to keep it in repair.

In making a claim, a person must prove all the following elements by a fair preponderance of the evidence:

1) that the injured person gave the required statutory notice of injury;

2) that the road where the injury occurred was one that the municipality and not some other person or entity, had a duty to maintain or repair;

3) that there was a defect in the road;

4) that the municipality had notice of the defect;

5) that the municipality failed to exercise reasonable care to remedy said defect; and

6) that the defect was the sole proximate cause of the injuries – that is, no other cause was a substantial factor in causing the injuries.

All these elements must be proven.

Just as in cases where someone falls on a sidewalk, the applicable statute in Connecticut states that an action can only be brought to recover damages caused by a defective road if the injured person provides written notice of the injury. This notice must include a general description of the injury, the cause, the time, and the place of its occurrence. This notice must be given within ninety days of the injury to a selectman or clerk of the town, city, or borough bound to keep the road in repair.

Of course, giving notice doesn't mean you are required to file a case, but doing so is necessary to preserving your claim for a road injury. No notice, no case.

Legal Malpractice

Cases in which someone is injured on a sidewalk or road are unfortunately ripe for legal malpractice. It's all too easy to miss that ninety-day window in which notice is required, but the statute is unforgiving. We have brought claims against lawyers who failed to give proper notice in a timely fashion. If your lawyer didn't give notice or gave improper notice, you may have a legal malpractice claim.

Loss of Consortium

Can a spouse recover losses by filing an independent claim under an auto policy?

This is an important question, and one I see arising more and more frequently in my cases. I trace this phenomenon to Connecticut's irresponsibly low auto insurance coverage minimums, which are as follows:

1. $20,000 for injury to or death of a person,

2. $40,000 for injury to or death of more than one person in any accident, and

3. $10,000 for property damage (CGS §§ 38a-335 and 14-112(a)).

To put this in context, let me tell you a story. A woman is driving her car. She's in her lane. Suddenly a man who is staring at his cell phone while driving crosses the centerline and hits her head-on. She sustains multiple fractures in her legs and face and requires emergency surgery. She spends weeks in the hospital, and after she's released, she needs home rehabilitation. As is far too common, the guy who chose to Snapchat his girlfriend over preserving everyone's safety has only a state minimum policy of 20/40. He has no other assets to attach: no house, no money in the bank. Nothing.

As a result of the accident, the victim's husband has to take family and medical leave to care for her. He spends countless hours taking her to doctor's appointments and doing the household tasks she used to do. In this case, the husband may want to make a claim for loss of consortium.

Loss of consortium is a suit by a spouse for the loss of the affection, dependence, and companionship that he has suffered. Damages for loss of consortium include both past and future losses. "Consortium" includes affection, society, companionship, and physical intimacies of the spousal relationship. A 20/40 policy means the insurance company is limited to only having to pay out $20,000 per person and $40,000 per wreck. For example, if there was a passenger in the woman's car, the total the insurance company would have to pay out is $40,000: $20,000 to the driver and $20,000 to the passenger. Can the husband recover even though he was not in the car, but suffered a compensable loss as a direct result of the driver choosing to violate road safety rules?

The answer is a very unsatisfactory "no." The amount of coverage available to both the injured person and her spouse is only $20,000.

A plaintiff asserting a claim for a loss of consortium cannot recover an independent "per person" recovery under an automobile insurance policy. Connecticut courts hold that a loss of consortium is a derivative claim. If you like reading such things, the leading Connecticut case on this issue is *Izzo v. Colonial Penn Ins Co.*, 203 Conn. 305 (1987). Most of all, what you'll notice if you read this case is that the limits in 1983 were also 20/40. In the face of massive medical inflation over the past thirty-three years, these minimal limits remain in place.

Further, the insurance companies limit their liability in their auto policies. The standard clause in the policy defining the "per person" liability limit as "all damages arising from that person's bodily injuries" also precludes recovery for a loss of consortium. This is nothing more than profits over people.

Suing a Connecticut Town or School

Over the years, I have brought several cases against towns and boards of education for failing to follow safety rules. Perhaps no area of Connecticut personal injury law is as muddled and confusing as bringing a claim against a city, town, or school board.

Towns and schools can be sued in Connecticut, but it's not as straightforward as suing a person or corporation. Towns and school boards can assert the special defense of governmental immunity – meaning they can't be sued. I'm going to explain some issues that may arise concerning governmental immunity, but this is by no means a comprehensive discussion.

Discretionary Act Immunity

A town employee, while working on behalf of the public, cannot be found liable for negligent acts or omissions if those acts or omissions were the result of an exercise of the employee's judgment and discretion. This immunity protects both the innocent employee and the one who did not follow safety rules. For example, a board of education that decides between two actions is using its discretion and is therefore immune from suit. This allows government employees to make decisions without fear of being second-guessed in the courtroom.

Ministerial Acts

By contrast, town and school employees can be sued for performing or failing to perform acts over which they have no discretion. These are known as ministerial acts. Ministerial acts are those duties which the public employee must perform in a prescribed manner, without the exercise of judgment or discretion. Courts have found activities such as driving to be ministerial acts because town employees and police officers have no choice but to follow the road safety rules to prevent car accidents.

Identifiable Victim

A governmental immunity defense is not ironclad. One exception to governmental immunity occurs when the injured person is an "identifiable victim." A person is an identifiable victim if it should have been apparent to the employee that their actions or their failure to act would be likely to place the plaintiff in imminent danger. There are three elements to the identifiable victim exception, and anyone who makes this assertion must prove:

1. That the injured person was an identifiable victim with respect to the claims of negligence against the defendant;

2. That the harm which the injured person experienced was imminent when the employee acted or failed to act; and

3. That it was apparent to the employee that their conduct was likely to subject the injured person to the particular harm alleged.

These three elements are interrelated. For example, if a school knows a student is being bullied but takes no action to stop the bullying, the school may trigger the identifiable victim exception to immunity.

Identifiable Class of Victims

In addition to the identifiable victim exception to immunity, there is the identifiable class of victims exception. The identifiable class of victims exception requires that an attorney prove the following:

1. That the injured person was a member of an identifiable class of victims with respect to their claims of negligence against the defendant;

2. That the harm that they experienced was imminent when the employee acted or failed to act; and

3. That it was apparent to the employee that the employee's conduct was likely to subject the injured person to the particular harm alleged.

A member of an identifiable class of victims may be a student at a public school who was required to be at school and who was exposed to a risk while at school. For instance, if a school knows that certain students are allergic to peanuts but serves them cookies containing peanuts, those students are members of an identifiable class of victims.

The bottom line is that if you ever find yourself having a claim against a town or a board of education, it is important that you immediately contact a personal injury attorney. In addition to immunity issues, there are also potential notices that must be given to a town very soon after an injury or death. Your lawyer needs to make sure that notice is properly given, a complaint is properly pleaded, and discovery is conducted in a way that prevents your case from being dismissed. This area of law is full of traps for the unwary.

Dog Bites

Dog bites can cause serious permanent injury or death. Even a "small" bite can lead to serious infection that results in surgery or hospitalization. Many of my dog bite cases begin with an owner saying, "Jojo (or whoever) would never bite anyone." But still, it happens.

I have been bitten by a dog on several occasions, including one time when a dog ripped me off my bicycle. It happens so quickly. Fortunately, the times I was bitten I've been okay, but other folks aren't so lucky.

Anyone who owns or keeps a dog is held strictly liable under our law for any damage caused by the dog. Strict liability does not depend on intent to harm. A person is liable if something happens – in this case a dog bite – whether or not they did anything wrong.

Connecticut Dog Bite Law

Under the Connecticut General Statutes, "If any dog does any damage to either the body or property of any person, the owner or keeper shall be liable for such damage, except when such damage has been occasioned to the body or property of a person who, at the time such damage was sustained, was committing a trespass or other tort, or was teasing, tormenting or abusing such dog." C.G.S. § 22-357.

A "keeper" of a dog means someone other than the owner who harbors or has possession of any dog. In a dog bite case, the attorney must prove: 1) that the defendants were the owners or keepers of a dog, 2) that the dog hurt the plaintiff's body or property, and 3) that neither of the exceptions applies.

Exceptions To Strict Liability

There are two exceptions to strict liability for dog bites. The first is that the person bitten by the dog was committing a "trespass or other tort." A tort is a wrongful act, so "committing a trespass or other tort" means more than merely entering the property or the area where the dog was. Rather, this means that the injured person entered the property or area to harm a person or property. If a dog bites a home invader, then there is no liability.

The second exception is for cases in which someone was "teasing, tormenting, or abusing" the dog. Teasing, tormenting or abusing a dog means engaging in actions that would naturally annoy or irritate a dog and provoke it to retaliate.

Injuries by Cats

I've been injured by a cat. Can I sue?

In high school, a classmate got cat scratch fever. One day he was healthy, the next day he was in a coma. He remained in the coma for weeks, and he nearly died. His doctors feared permanent brain damage. Fortunately, he survived, but this was all the result of being scratched by a cat.

There are lots of dog bite cases, but many fewer cases about cats – probably because many cat attacks result in minimal injuries. Those cases are simply not worth bringing. But what about the cases in which someone suffers significant injuries? The Connecticut Supreme Court in *Allen v. Cox* held that when a cat has a propensity to attack other cats, knowledge of that propensity may render the owner liable for injuries that are reasonably foreseeable as a result of such behavior. This is the most important case in cat injury law in Connecticut.

In sum, if you've been severely injured by a cat, the only way to know whether you have a claim is to know the cat's behavioral history.

Bed Bugs

Bed bugs are nasty.

Spending a night in a hotel room should not result in welts, the destruction of your furniture at home, and a weeks-long fumigation process. Shouldn't happen. But bed bugs can happen even at a meticulous five-star hotel. How? A traveler unwittingly brushes up against bed bug eggs on an airplane, bus, or train seat and carries them into their hotel. Just like that, the hotel now has a bed bug problem.

According to the Centers For Disease Control, "bed bugs hide during the day in places such as seams of mattresses, box springs, bed frames, headboards, dresser tables, inside cracks or crevices, behind wallpaper, or any other clutter or objects around a bed. Bed bugs have been shown to be able to travel over 100 feet in a night but tend to live within 8 feet of where people sleep."

The good news is that bed bugs are not known to spread disease. The bad news is that I wouldn't wish them on anyone. They can create major headaches.

Is a hotel responsible for bed bug bites? Can I sue the hotel?

The answer – like the answer to so many things – is *maybe*.

We have successfully brought bed bug claims against hotels. We have also declined a number of cases. What we look for is evidence that the hotel knew of a problem and failed to act. If a hotel doesn't know or doesn't have any reason to know it has bed bugs, than it's possible there is no claim. For example, the traveler before you brought in bed bugs. They were hiding under some wallpaper. You hit the unlucky lottery and are bitten. Upon learning of this, the hotel treats the premises for bed bugs.

Hotels can't be willfully blind to bed bugs. Bed bugs are a foreseeable risk to their customers. Hotels have to have inspection and treatment procedures. They must take actions to prevent bed bug bites.

When we bring a case, we look at any prior publicly available reports – such as complaints to the Department of Health, town, or lawsuits – in order to try to determine how a hotel handles bed bugs.

If our investigation reveals that the hotel knew or should have known about bed bugs and failed to act properly, than the hotel may be held responsible for the damages caused by their failure. The hotel may be liable to cover medical bills, damage to property, pain, and anxiety.

Injured While Playing Sports

In Connecticut, recreational sports have made it to our highest court: *Jaworski v. Kiernan*, 241 Conn. 399 (1997).

During a coed recreational soccer game, Kiernan made contact with Jaworski while Jaworski was shielding the soccer ball. As a result, Jaworski suffered an injury to her left anterior cruciate ligament, which caused a 15 percent permanent partial disability of her left knee.

Jaworski sued Kiernan for her injuries, claiming among other things that Kiernan should be found liable for negligence because his actions violated league rules. The Supreme Court disagreed and offered this analysis of the game of soccer:

"Soccer, while not as violent a sport as football, is nevertheless replete with occasions when the participants make contact with one another during the normal course of the game. When two soccer players vie for control of the ball, the lower limbs are especially vulnerable to injury. If a player seeks to challenge another player who has possession of the ball or seeks to prevent another player from gaining possession of the ball, the resulting contact could reasonably be foreseen to result in injury to either player."

The court went on to find that the defendant could not be held liable for negligence, but only deliberate, willful, or reckless conduct:

"A final public policy concern that influences our decision is our desire to stem the possible flood of litigation that might result from adopting simple negligence as the standard of care to be utilized in athletic contests. If simple negligence were adopted as the standard of care, every punter with whom contact is made, every midfielder high-sticked, every basketball player fouled, every batter struck by a pitch, and every hockey player tripped would have the ingredients for a lawsuit if injury resulted. When the number of athletic events taking place in Connecticut over the course of a year is considered, there exists the potential for a surfeit of lawsuits when it becomes known that simple negligence, based on an inadvertent violation of a contest rule, will suffice as a ground for recovery for an athletic injury. This should not be encouraged."

If you have been injured playing sports, whether or not you can sue in Connecticut will depend on how your injury occurred. Every situation is unique, but the general rule is that a basic violation of the rules of the game is insufficient to make a claim.

Miscarriage After a Car Accident

Last week I was driving on I-84 when traffic suddenly came to a crawl. Emergency vehicles sped past, and I was shocked to see a visibly pregnant woman lying on the side of the road beside her broken vehicle, clutching her stomach.

As a father, getting into a car accident with my pregnant wife numbered among my worst nightmares during her pregnancy. I know the pain a miscarriage can cause all too well. It is awful.

My sincere hope is that this woman and her baby are both fine and thriving, but it got me thinking: What happens if a car accident causes a miscarriage in Connecticut?

Accidents can cause miscarriages. Some very old Connecticut cases do not award damages for the wrongful death of a fetus. There is a case that dates back to 1939 (*Sullivan v. Connecticut Company*, 7 Conn. Supp. 35) in which a trolley in New Haven came to an abrupt stop, causing a woman who was two months pregnant to miscarry. The trolley company was found liable for her damages, but only to the extent of the injuries she had personally suffered. For example, the court noted that the plaintiff had been confined to the hospital for ten days, suffered pain and discomfort, and incurred medical expenses. Even though the court found that the plaintiff had indeed lost her pregnancy as a result of the defendant's driver's negligence, she was not awarded damages for a wrongful death.

In another case from the 1930s, a woman alleged that the defendant had negligently served her a sandwich that contained glass. She suffered emotional distress that she claimed ultimately resulted in a miscarriage. (*Gannon v. S.S. Kresge Co.*, 114 Conn. 36 (1931).) Again, the plaintiff was awarded damages for her emotional and physical suffering, but apparently not for the wrongful death of her child.

Science has come a long way in the past century, and we know things through ultrasounds and fetal monitoring that the courts in *Sullivan* and *Gannon* could not have imagined. Of course, the law has also evolved since that time.

Fast forward to 2011, when a doctor in Stamford was sued for the wrongful death of a twenty-two-week-old fetus. The doctor was accused of negligently rupturing fetal membranes while removing an intrauterine device. This case was pretty big news because Connecticut has not considered whether someone can be found liable for the wrongful death of a fetus. Unfortunately the case settled, which means that this is still an open question.

So if someone is injured in Connecticut and suffers a miscarriage as a result, can that person recover for the wrongful death of the fetus? The courts haven't said. These kinds of cases are complicated. A plaintiff would have to prove that the fetus was viable and would have survived birth. This would involve the testimony of multiple experts.

As a firm, we believe in the dignity of life and that wrongdoers should be held accountable for their actions. If a car accident causes a miscarriage in Connecticut, we believe that the defendant should be civilly liable for wrongful death.

Depositions

So you've been hurt because someone didn't follow safety rules, and then the insurance company made you lowball offers, forcing you to file suit in order to be treated fairly. Now you are in the litigation process and they want to take your deposition. This post explains some of the basics of depositions in personal injury cases.

What is a deposition?

A deposition is your opportunity to ask the other party questions under oath in real time. A deposition is taken in front of a court reporter who swears in the witness and transcribes everything said. After the deposition, the court reporter will give you the opportunity to purchase the transcript, which you can then use in court as an exhibit.

How long does a deposition take?

This depends on a lot of factors. Generally, depositions of our clients are about ninety minutes. In more complicated cases, depositions can last several hours. Good defense attorneys know what to ask, how to ask it, and how to avoid unnecessary questioning.

What does a deposition cost?

The cost of a deposition is directly dependent on the court reporting company used because each company charges different rates. Our lawyers handle personal injury cases on a contingency fee – meaning they are not paid hourly for their time in a deposition. Generally court reporter fees and transcripts run anywhere from $400 to $1000 depending on the length of the deposition.

How are depositions scheduled?

Scheduling a deposition requires sending the other party a Notice of Deposition detailing the place, time, and date of the deposition. The best practice is to reach out to the opposing counsel and the court reporter to inquire about availability prior to preparing the Notice of Deposition. This can avoid scheduling problems.

Can they ask me to bring documents to the deposition?

Yes, you can be required to bring certain documents to the deposition if you are served with a subpoena duces tecum listing the desired documents and attaching it to the Notice of Deposition. In a personal injury case in Connecticut, it is rare for a plaintiff to have to bring documents to a deposition because all documents get turned over pursuant to standard discovery.

What kinds of questions can I be asked?

Generally defense counsel asks questions about the plaintiff's background – things like work and school history; prior medical injuries; how the accident that gave rise to the lawsuit happened; and treatment history. Defense counsel can ask any question so long as it doesn't infringe on attorney-client privilege and is reasonably likely to lead to admissible evidence in court.

Can a deposition help to settle my case?

Yes. Cases often settle after a deposition. Keep in mind that when you make a claim, the insurance company has no idea who you are or how you will present to a jury or a judge, but we know that who you are influences a fact finder. This is the insurance company's opportunity to meet you. After a good deposition, the insurance company may realize their best option is to pay you.

Why do defendants take depositions?

In addition to wanting to meet you, defense attorneys have several reasons for taking a deposition.

Discovery: Depositions are a great way to figure out what happened. For example, after any question they can ask, "Do you have any proof of that?" If you answer, "Yes," then they can follow up with questions that will allow them to track down the proof. On the other hand, if you answer "No," then they know that particular issue will boil down to the witness's credibility. Furthermore, if the witness attempts to produce proof at a later date, they may have grounds to exclude the proof from evidence.

Locking Down Facts/Positions: Because a deposition is taken under oath, it is a great opportunity to lock down the other party's positions or version of facts for particular issues.

Cross Examination: At trial, the general rule is that you do not want to ask a hostile (non-friendly) witness a question you do not already know the answer to. Taking the other party's deposition allows them to ask the more open-ended questions they might typically avoid at trial because they don't know the answer. Come trial, a lawyer knows the answer and can use the answer in cross examination.

Where do depositions take place?

It takes place either at your lawyer's office, at the office of the defense lawyer, or at a neutral office such as that of a court reporter. Deponents aren't forced to travel more than 30 miles from their residence to be deposed, and parties usually reach an agreement on location in advance.

Will my deposition be videotaped?

Maybe. Depositions can be videotaped, and we regularly do so, but there must be written notice of the intent to videotape. So you'll know in advance of the deposition whether or not a video will be taken.

In conclusion, your lawyer should prepare you for the ins and outs of the deposition in your case. Witness preparation is extremely important. It is vital that you walk into the deposition feeling confident. This is one of the most critical parts of your case, and it may be your only chance to tell your story.

Risks of Trial

The goal of the legal system is to produce certain and repeatable results. Two cases with similar facts should reach similar outcomes regardless of who the judge, lawyer, clerks or jurors are. This is one of the most noble and basic notions in law: justice should be blind.

But the law feels anything other than predictable. Ask any lawyer worth their salt. They'll tell you they've lost cases they thought were slam dunks and won cases they thought were sure losers. A case feels like a roller coaster for even the most seasoned of attorneys. One ruling, one judge, one juror, or one small fact can change everything.

So here you are. You have been seriously injured in a trucking wreck. You ask your friends for advice, you do your online research, and you meet with several lawyers before deciding on the one you believe to be best suited for your case. The lawyer has results, a record, and a commitment to you. You feel like you're in good hands.

For much of your case, it's all going along as your attorney predicted. The only offers the insurance company makes are the lowball ones that your lawyer has warned you about. You've been told the strengths and weaknesses of your case, and you get it. Nothing is certain. You know someone wronged you and that you've been hurt. You trust in your lawyer and you know she's working as hard as she can to win your case. But at the end of the day, you know the system is human and humans are unpredictable.

Risks of a Personal Injury Trial

1) Losing

If the jury comes back with a defense verdict, that means you lost. Losing means you get zero dollars. Nothing. Years of angst, days off from work, meetings with your lawyer and it's all for nothing. Even with the strongest possible case, there is always some chance you lose. Recently I was speaking with a judge who said that several recent car accident cases – where the defendants admitted they were responsible for the accidents – came back as defense verdicts from a jury.

Losing is always a risk.

2) Receiving Less Money Than Offered for Settlement

The ultimate goal of any plaintiff's lawyer is to beat the last offer from the insurance company at trial. There are only two numbers that matter in a personal injury case – what a jury will award you and what an insurance company will pay you. If you go to trial and the jury awards more money than the insurance company's last offer, it's a win. If you are awarded less money by a jury than the insurance company was offering, it is a loss.

Receiving less money is a risk of a personal injury trial.

3) You Owe Your Lawyer Costs

Connecticut has two kinds of fee agreements. One is a fee waiver agreement in which the client waives the statutory fee structure and gives the lawyer a third of the gross settlement regardless of how large that settlement is. In exchange, the client gets certainty that the lawyer will not pursue the client for costs in the event of a loss. The other kind of fee agreement – a statutory fee agreement – makes the client responsible for costs in the event of a loss. Costs could include expert fees, deposition costs, court costs, and other costs as explained in your fee agreement.

Sometimes costs can be high. If you lose, you may have to reimburse your lawyer. You should have this conversation at the beginning of your relationship with any lawyer and demand to be constantly updated about litigation costs and projected costs.

4) You Owe the Defendant Costs

After winning at trial, a defendant can file a bill of costs. The defendant can get reimbursed costs for trial, witness fees, depositions, experts, and other such costs pursuant to Connecticut General Statutes Sec. 52-257. Sometimes these costs can be in the thousands of dollars. Again, this is a discussion you should have with your lawyer prior to trial.

5) The Defendant Sues You

In Connecticut, a prevailing party in an action may bring a lawsuit for vexatious litigation or abuse of process. Essentially the claim is that there was no probable cause for you to have brought your claim. It is a high burden for a party to meet, but such claims are on the rise nationally and in Connecticut. Even if you didn't engage in vexatious litigation, it may cost you money to fight the claim.

Even winning is not without its risks. There are a few additional problems that may appear even if you prevail at trial.

1) Defendant May File a Motion for Remittitur

The defendant may file a motion for remittitur. Remittitur is a motion to reduce a jury verdict that the defendant believes is excessive. The judge may order the plaintiff to remit a portion of the award.

The remedy of remittitur is designed to cure an award of damages that is grossly excessive without the necessity of a new trial or an appeal. In some cases, an award by a jury is so completely out of line with the damages proven in the case that it is unconscionable. A motion for remittitur is brought under Connecticut Practice Book Section 16-35. The defendant can also attempt to seek a new trial on such grounds.

2) Defendant May Seek a Collateral Source Reduction

Connecticut General Statutes Sec. 52-255a allows a defendant to seek a collateral source reduction. Connecticut's collateral source statute reads as follows (in relevant part):

"In any civil action, whether in tort or in contract, wherein the claimant seeks to recover damages resulting from (1) personal injury or wrongful death ... and wherein liability is admitted or is determined by the trier of fact and damages are awarded to compensate the claimant, the court shall reduce the amount of such award which represents economic damages ... by an amount equal to the total of amounts determined to have been paid under subsection (b) of this section less the total of amounts determined to have been paid under subsection (c) of this section ...."

Thus, if a health insurance company pays benefits without rights of subrogation, there may be an offset entered. Of course, that offset is then offset again by the amount of health insurance premiums you have paid.

Collateral source reductions can take time for the parties to figure out and sometimes they result in hearings. These hearings may delay final judgment in a case by months.

3) Defendant May Appeal

A party generally has twenty days after the mailing of judgment to file an appeal in Connecticut. This can be extended several different ways, including through a motion to reargue. But if you win your case, the defendant can appeal. Appeals involve additional costs and can take a year or more to resolve and . If the defendant is successful, there will likely be a new trial, again, adding additional costs and delay. You have to pay experts to testify all over again.

4) Defendant May Go Bankrupt

There is always the possibility that a defendant or an insurance company may go bankrupt. This happens from time to time. In that case, your claim may be defeated in bankruptcy court and your judgment will be uncollectible. Bankruptcy can happen at any time in a case.

5) You May Have to Chase the Defendant for Money

If there is inadequate insurance to cover your judgment, you may have to seek wage, bank, and property executions to get paid. You may also have to file a lien on a defendant's real property. You may not see it for years, or you may not see it at all.

What You Can Do

All plaintiffs entering a court need to know all the possible outcomes for a case. From there, you should have frequent conversations with your attorney about the probability of those various outcomes. Some cases have to get tried, but other times settlement, mediation, or even arbitration may be a preferred means of resolving your personal injury case. We love to try cases, but it's because we prepare for trial that many of our cases can be resolved outside of the courthouse.

Personal Injury Mediation

The statistics tell us that 97 percent of Connecticut personal injury cases resolve prior to a jury trial, and sometimes even prior to filing suit. Mediation can be an effective way to resolve cases.

Mediation in Connecticut is a voluntary process in which the parties agree to sit down, discuss, and attempt to resolve their case with a neutral party. The neutral party is called a mediator. A mediator cannot force the parties to settle. All a mediator can do is attempt to facilitate settlement between the parties.

Personal injury mediators in Connecticut are frequently active or retired judges or attorneys with experience in personal injury litigation. The state of Connecticut judicial branch has a judicial mediation program that is free for litigants as of this writing. To participate in the judicial mediation program, the parties simply select a judge and schedule a mediation. Sometimes the parties choose to participate in private mediation instead, in which case they share the cost of a private mediator. No matter which route the litigants choose, both parties must agree to the mediator.

Choosing the right mediator is an important decision. Experienced Connecticut personal injury attorneys are effective at matching cases with the right mediator.

When does personal injury mediation happen?

The answer is, "It depends." I have successfully mediated cases prior to filing suit, and I have successfully mediated cases on the eve of trial. It often depends on the willingness of the parties to resolve the matter. Sometimes, legal issues need to be sorted out first so parties have a better understanding of the strengths and weaknesses of their case. Mediation can happen at any time.

Do I have to mediate my case?

No. Participation in the mediation process is voluntary. Sometimes cases can be resolved over a phone call, sometimes in a pretrial meeting with the judge, and sometimes during trial itself. Mediation is just one tool.

In my experience, mediating a case at the right time and with the right mediator can bring about a quick and effective resolution of a case. Mediation done properly is a lot of work. A case needs to be presented in a way that ensures the mediator understands the significance of the claims being made. Clients also have to understand the mediation process. It is much more than just relaying numbers back and- orth.

Arbitration

Arbitration is another effective means of resolving a personal injury case in Connecticut.

Private arbitration is a process by which the parties agree to have their case heard by a neutral fact finder. The fact finder then renders a decision that is binding on the parties. In Connecticut, arbitration happens by contract: the parties agree to the rules and agree to be bound by the ruling of the fact finder.

Arbitrations often require testimony and parties will agree to the admission of documents. In complicated cases, arbitration can last as long as several days. Where appropriate, however, cases may be taken on the papers, meaning that no testimony is required. Arbitrators in personal injury cases are usually respected and experienced personal injury attorneys or retired judges. Sometimes there is only one arbitrator, but parties may also agree to a three-arbitrator panel.

Court-ordered arbitration applies to cases in Connecticut with an anticipated value of under $50,000. Unlike private arbitration, court-ordered arbitration is both free and non-binding in the sense that either party can appeal the decision of the arbitrator and the case will proceed to trial. The purpose of court-ordered arbitration is to inform the parties of the potential outcome at trial and to encourage settlement.

What is the Difference Between Arbitration and Mediation?

Mediation in Connecticut personal injury cases is a voluntary process where the parties agree to a settlement. In a private arbitration, the arbitrator decides on an outcome in the same way that a judge or jury might.

Whether your case goes to arbitration will depend on many factors. Some cases are ripe for arbitration, which can result in a faster and cheaper resolution of a personal injury case. In other cases, a jury is more appropriate. Only an experienced attorney can help you make this decision.

Jury Selection

A jury is the conscience of the community. It is the most important role a citizen can play in our democracy.

The power of the juror's vote on a case is a great power. It impacts not only the parties to the case but the community, and what happens in the courtroom echoes throughout the state.

Juries decide how much we value life, whether or not safety rules matter, and whether accountability and personal responsibility matter.

How many jurors will sit on an injury case?

In Connecticut, we seat six jurors and two alternates. The alternates sit through all testimony. They only vote if one of the six jurors is excused.

How do you select a juror?

We select jurors by participating in a process called "voir dire." This is a phrase that means "to speak the truth," which is fitting because we ask jurors a lot of questions to learn more about them. Basically we want to ensure that any juror we seat is not only comfortable applying the facts we present to the law, but will take that responsibility seriously. Connecticut is unique because we have individual voir dire, which means that when we speak to potential jurors, it's one at time rather than in a group. However, the attorneys in a case may agree to box void dire, allowing them to interview a group of prospective jurors at once.

During void dire, each lawyer can strike four jurors for any legal reason. An example of an illegal reason would be dismissing someone on the basis of race. Other jurors can be removed for cause. Cause is simply a bias that would prevent the person from fulfilling their duties. For example, if a prospective juror states their belief that plaintiffs should never be awarded money in a lawsuit, or that plaintiffs should never receive money for pain and suffering, that juror would be removed for cause – in this case, their inability or unwillingness to follow Connecticut law.

Every juror is very important. We are grateful for all who serve.

Offers of Compromise

An offer of compromise is a pleading that gets filed with the court to settle a case for a specific amount of money. For example, if a plaintiff decides that she is willing to accept ten thousand dollars to settle her case, a ten-thousand-dollar offer of compromise could be filed with the court. If the defendant believes the offer of compromise is reasonable, they could accept it and the case will end.

When can an offer of compromise be filed?

In a normal personal injury case (a car accident, dog bite, wrongful death, etc.), an offer of compromise can be filed from 180 from the date on which the other side was served with a complaint. An offer of compromise cannot be filed before 180 days in a normal personal injury case, or before 365 days in a medical malpractice case.

What is the effect of an offer of compromise?

In any personal injury case, the determination of when, how, and for how much to file an offer of compromise is an important strategic decision. If the offer of compromise is filed between six and eighteen months of the date of the service of a complaint, and if the defendant rejects that offer, then any amount the plaintiff recovers in court in excess of the offer will accrue interest. For example, let's say an offer of compromise was $10,000 and that the defendant rejected this offer. A jury later awards the plaintiff $30,000. There is a $20,000 difference between the offer of compromise and the jury award. The court will apply interest to that $20,000 at the rate of 8% from the date on which the offer of compromise was first filed. An offer of compromise can add significant value to a case, particularly when dealing with high-value cases.

Connecticut Offer of Compromise Statute

> Sec. 52-192a. Offer of compromise by plaintiff. Acceptance by defendant. Amount and computation of interest. (a) Except as provided in subsection (b) of this section, after commencement of any civil action based upon contract or seeking the recovery of money damages, whether or not other relief is sought, the plaintiff may, not earlier than one hundred eighty days after service of process is made upon the defendant in such action but not later than thirty days before trial, file with the clerk of the court a written offer of compromise signed by the plaintiff or the plaintiff's attorney, directed to the defendant or the defendant's attorney, offering to settle the claim underlying the action for a sum certain. For the purposes of this section, such plaintiff includes a

counterclaim plaintiff under section 8-132. The plaintiff shall give notice of the offer of compromise to the defendant's attorney or, if the defendant is not represented by an attorney, to the defendant himself or herself. Within thirty days after being notified of the filing of the offer of compromise and prior to the rendering of a verdict by the jury or an award by the court, the defendant or the defendant's attorney may file with the clerk of the court a written acceptance of the offer of compromise agreeing to settle the claim underlying the action for the sum certain specified in the plaintiff's offer of compromise. Upon such filing and the receipt by the plaintiff of such sum certain, the plaintiff shall file a withdrawal of the action with the clerk and the clerk shall record the withdrawal of the action against the defendant accordingly. If the offer of compromise is not accepted within thirty days and prior to the rendering of a verdict by the jury or an award by the court, the offer of compromise shall be considered rejected and not subject to acceptance unless refiled. Any such offer of compromise and any acceptance of the offer of compromise shall be included by the clerk in the record of the case.

(b) In the case of any action to recover damages resulting from personal injury or wrongful death, whether in tort or in contract, in which it is alleged that such injury or death resulted from the negligence of a health care provider, the plaintiff may, not earlier than three hundred sixty-five days after service of process is made upon the defendant in such action, file with the clerk of the court a written offer of compromise pursuant to subsection (a) of this section and, if the offer of compromise is not accepted within sixty days and prior to the rendering of a verdict by the jury or an award by the court, the offer of compromise shall be considered rejected and not subject to acceptance unless refiled.

(c) After trial the court shall examine the record to determine whether the plaintiff made an offer of compromise which the defendant failed to accept. If the court ascertains from the record that the plaintiff has recovered an amount equal to or greater than the sum certain specified in the plaintiff's offer of compromise, the court shall add to the amount so recovered eight per cent annual interest on said amount, except in the case of a counterclaim plaintiff under section 8-132, the court shall add to the amount so recovered eight per cent annual interest on the difference between the amount so recovered and the sum certain specified in the counterclaim plaintiff's offer of compromise. The interest shall be computed from the date the complaint in the civil action or application under section 8-132 was filed with the court if the offer of compromise was filed not later than eighteen months from the filing of such complaint or application. If such offer was filed later than eighteen months from the date of filing of the complaint or application, the interest shall be computed from the date the offer of compromise was filed. The court may award reasonable attorney's fees in an amount not to exceed three hundred fifty dollars, and shall render judgment accordingly. This section shall not be interpreted to abrogate the contractual rights of any party concerning the recovery of attorney's fees in accordance with the provisions of any written contract between the parties to the action.

Trial

Whether you're talking about movies, television, or the latest legal thriller, the media tends to fixate on only one aspect of law: trial. No one has yet sold a screenplay about the attorney who drafted the most amazing trust ever.

Personal injury cases can be tried before a judge or a jury. However, they are most commonly tried before a jury. The following are the typical stages of a jury trial in Connecticut.

Voir Dire

I cover the process of void dire in a previous section on jury selection. For the purposes of this section, just know that the first step of a jury trial is jury selection.

Opening Statements

Opening statements are the first opportunity for all parties to introduce their respective cases to the jury. Opening statements are not evidence. Their purpose is to allow the parties to orient the jury to issues they may hear in the case. They are the story of the case. The plaintiff gives the first opening statement, followed by the defendant. Opening statements can vary in length depending on the evidence that will be presented at trial. Lawyers do not argue in opening statements.

Plaintiff Case in Chief

The plaintiff must present his or her case. In an injury case, the plaintiff may call all or some of the following people: eyewitnesses, police officers, records keepers, doctors, family members, the plaintiff, expert witnesses, and other fact witnesses. The plaintiff has the sole burden to prove their case by a preponderance of the evidence. During this time the defense may cross examine any of the plaintiff's witnesses.

Defense Case

The defense does not have to call any witnesses. Unlike the plaintiff, the defendant does not have to prove anything. This is what we mean when we say that the plaintiff has the burden of proof. Still, the defendant may choose to call its own experts, fact witnesses, or any other person useful to explaining its case. The plaintiff has the opportunity to cross examine defense witnesses.

Rebuttal Witnesses

If the defendant has presented evidence, the plaintiff may choose to call witnesses to rebut the defendant's case.

Evidence

Evidence is the information and materials a party introduces to support their position. Evidence comes in the form of testimony – both live and recorded – documents, and pictures. When an attorney calls a witness or asks to enter an exhibit, that attorney is introducing evidence.

Closing Arguments

Unlike in opening statements, attorneys are permitted to argue the evidence in closing argument. This is when attorneys will put the evidence in context and explain its meaning to the jury. Closing arguments are not evidence, and they must be based on only the evidence admitted during trial. Nothing new is introduced at closing argument.

The plaintiff goes first, followed by the defendant, and then the plaintiff has one last opportunity to rebut what the defense has said in closing arguments.

Deliberations

After closing arguments, the judge will instruct the jury on the law. This is called a jury charge. Once the jury is charged, they will go into a private room and deliberate. Juries have as long as they like to deliberate. Sometimes they submit written questions to the court seeking clarification of their charge. When a jury reaches a decision, it is called a verdict.

Verdict

The jury foreperson gives a note to the jury clerk stating that a verdict has been reached. The jury then returns to the courtroom and presents the verdict to the court clerk. The court clerk then reads the verdict. Then judgment enters and the case is over.

This is the basic structure of a Connecticut personal injury trial, though of course many pages could be written about any of these stages.

Liens

So you've been in a car accident and you've mentioned to a friend that you're talking to an attorney. Your friend says, "Why bother? Isn't any money you recover going to be eaten up by liens?" And suddenly you're not sure.

A lien is an amount of money that must be paid to someone else after you receive a settlement or a judgment. For example, if you receive $10,000 from a settlement but there is a $2,000 lien on your file, then you are entitled to receive $8,000. Basically, it's a bill that must be paid.

Being in a car accident wasn't something you planned for. Maybe it has made a tough financial situation nearly impossible. The last thing you want to think about is owing someone else money. However, this book would not be complete without at least some discussion of liens.

What liens are not allowed in a personal injury case in Connecticut?

Generally speaking, if a private insurance company has paid for your medical costs, they are not entitled to recover those costs from you or the person who caused your injury. So if you've been in a car accident and have required surgery, and your insurance company covered that surgery to the tune of $100,000, Connecticut does not allow your insurance company to put a $100,000 lien on your file. Conn. Gen. Stat. Sec. 52-225c.

Of course there are some big exceptions to this rule – including self-funded ERISA plans and Medicaid – so don't put the book down just yet.

Medicare

Who is allowed to place a lien on a personal injury case in Connecticut? In a word, Medicare.

If you are receiving Medicare benefits for your injury, then Medicare has a right to place a lien on any amount you recover. In fact, your attorney is required to notify Medicare that you are seeking recovery from the person who caused your injuries so that Medicare can evaluate your case for repayment. 42 U.S.C. §1395y(b).

You may be thinking: so why tell Medicare in the first place? Well, because the United States can sue for double the amount up to six years later if they don't get their money in the first place, and no one wants that. 28 U.S.C. 2415(a).

When you are over sixty-five and on Medicare, every penny matters. You live on a fixed income, and sometimes you have to choose between buying food or paying for prescription medications. The good news is that sometimes your attorney can negotiate with Medicare to significantly reduce the lien.

So, are all Medicare plans allowed to lien a personal injury file?

No. That would be too simple.

If the insurance covering your treatment is a Medicare supplemental health plan – otherwise known as Medi-Gap insurance–then there is no right no recovery. Why? Because supplemental Medicare plans are not really Medicare plans, but private health insurance that is used to complement Medicare coverage. Remember that in Connecticut, the general rule is that private insurance providers may not recover their costs. Conn. Gen. Stat. Sec. 52-225c.

What about Medicare Advantage plans? Can they place a lien on my file?

We don't know. This is a question that Connecticut courts haven't fully addressed. There are good arguments against paying such a lien, but there is also unfavorable case law from other states that may influence a Connecticut court.

In short, Medicare Advantage plans are private insurance plans that are approved by Medicare. Federal law (42 U.S.C. §1395mm(e)(4)) authorizes these private insurers to recover costs from their insured, and many have placed this right to recovery in their contracts. But are these contractual provisions valid under Connecticut law, considering that we don't allow private insurers to recover their costs?

We simply don't know. It's not clear whether the federal law is intended to override state law. This is a question that your attorney will need to evaluate because if your Medicare Advantage contract does not include the language to permit recovery, case closed. They cannot lien your file. But if the contract does include that language, then your attorney must consider how to proceed.

Of course, as with Medicare, it is sometimes possible for your attorney to negotiate and significantly reduce a Medicare Advantage lien. We don't take Medicare Advantage Liens at face value. Many of them are bogus liens.

Medicaid

If you've been hurt in a car accident and you're a recipient of Medicaid, the last thing you want to hear is that Medicaid may lien some of your recovery. You may be a single parent, raising young children and struggling to make ends meet. We understand. We have many clients in your position. It's hard to make ends meet in Connecticut, and many people here receive assistance in the form of Husky Insurance. However, you should know that state and federal law give Medicaid the right to recover related medical costs.

Medicaid was created in 1965. It is a joint program between the state and federal governments to provide assistance to those who struggle to pay medical expenses. Each state administers its program for its citizens. Every Connecticut recipient of Medicaid has agreed to allow Medicaid to recover medical costs caused by third parties. Conn. Gen. Stat. Sec. 17b-265. In fact, if you're a Medicaid recipient, the state has the automatic right to directly pursue the person responsible for your injuries—this is called subrogation. In Connecticut, when a person has subrogation rights, that person also has the right to place a lien on a recovery.

There is some good news. Medicaid is only entitled to lien the portion of a recovery related to medical costs. In addition, sometimes Medicaid does not even put liens on Connecticut personal injury cases. And often times when they do, we negotiate a reduction.

SAGA Cash Assistance Liens

If you are over the age of eighteen and you have received benefits "under the state supplement program, medical assistance program, aid to families with dependent children program, temporary family assistance program or state-administered general assistance program," then the state may place a lien on your personal injury case. Conn. Gen. Stat. Sec. 17b-94. The amount of the lien can be the full amount of the benefits received **or** fifty percent of the recovery after certain litigation costs are subtracted, **whichever is less**.

Prison Liens

Some folks think that after they have done their time, they have paid their debt to society. Then they learn that society will send them another bill.

If you have been incarcerated within the past twenty years, the state may lien your case to recoup its costs. Conn. Gen. Stat. Sec. 18-85b. This lien would take priority over any lien for state assistance, and it would be equal to the full cost of incarceration **or** fifty percent of the recovery after certain litigation costs are subtracted, **whichever is less**. These liens are commonly called incarceration liens.

If you're concerned about a lien on your personal injury case, it's important to speak with an attorney so that you fully understand your rights. In this book we speak in general terms, but every case is unique and that's where trusted counsel can help. One of the best things you can do is to let your attorney know if you were incarcerated or have received cash assistance. Different rules apply in wrongful death cases.

Legal Malpractice

Legal malpractice is the term for negligence by an attorney that causes harm to a client.

A person making a legal malpractice claim must prove that the attorney's acts were not merely the result of poor strategy, but that they were the result of errors that no reasonably prudent attorney would make.

When you hire an attorney, ask whether they carry legal malpractice insurance. I have done hundreds if not thousands of potential client interviews, but I have never been asked about my insurance. Connecticut lawyers are not required to carry or disclose whether they carry insurance. I carry malpractice insurance to protect my clients.

An Overview

The practice of law is complicated and lawyers can screw up in a number of ways. The most common errors that lawyers make are failing to file cases or notices in time. This is called blowing a statute of limitations. When a lawyer fails to file notice or a case, this costs the client their claim. For example, if an attorney failed to give a town notice of a sidewalk or road defect within 90 days of an injury, the client cannot bring a claim to recover for their injuries. This may give rise to a legal malpractice action.

In a legal malpractice action, the client must prove:

1) there was an attorney-client relationship;

2) the attorney departed from the standard of professional care owed to protect the client's legal interests in that matter; and

3) this departure caused harm to the client.

Attorney-Client Relationship

An attorney-client relationship can be proven by the existence of a fee agreement. It can also be proven through an admission by the attorney of such a relationship. Failing to have a fee agreement can be an ethical violation for an attorney.

The Case within a Case

A simple mistake does not give rise to legal malpractice. Rather, the mistake must result in harm. A person seeking to prove legal malpractice must prove that it was more likely than not that they would have prevailed in the original case, but for the attorney's mistake. This often is referred to as "a case within a case."

For example, if your lawyer blew the statute of limitations on a case that you would have lost, there is no claim for legal malpractice because logically, you were not actually harmed by the attorney's error.

If you're considering bringing a legal malpractice action, you need to hire a lawyer who understands both the responsibilities of lawyers and how to win an underlying injury case.

When we prosecute legal malpractice cases against attorneys who have screwed up, I hire and consult with expert attorneys. I am also called upon by other attorneys to serve as an expert witness.

Dram Shop Notice Malpractice

If a person leaves a bar, drives while intoxicated, and causes your car accident, the bar may be responsible for damages of up to $250,000 if they negligently served the driver alcohol. They may be liable for more if their service was considered reckless. A lawyer must give notice of a dram shop claim within 120 days of the date of the injury. In the case of a death or incapacity, notice must be filed within 180 days. If notice is not filed, then a claim cannot be made against the bar for damages.

My Lawyer Shouldn't Have Settled My Case

Missing a statute of limitations isn't the only way to commit malpractice. Sometimes clients believe they received inadequate counsel about a settlement. Do you feel like you didn't get a good settlement? Or that your attorney failed to explain to you the terms of the settlement? Do you regret settling your case?

Connecticut law favors private resolution of claims through settlements. Attorneys giving advice to clients as to whether to accept or reject offers of settlement are still required to employ that same skill, knowledge, and diligence with which they pursue all other legal tasks.

The Connecticut Civil Jury Instruction on this issue reads as follows:

"In advising a client concerning settlement, the attorney must exercise that degree of learning and skill which the average and ordinarily prudent attorney in that line of practice in Connecticut would apply under all the relevant circumstances. Consequently, the plaintiff [in a settlement malpractice case] must prove, by a preponderance of the evidence, not only that the defendant rendered certain settlement advice which the plaintiff followed to his financial detriment, but also that the advice given to (him/her) fell below the standard for lawyers in that field of practice in Connecticut."

In other words, simple regret is not enough.

Your attorney may have committed malpractice if:

1. They failed to investigate the personal assets of the defendant and advised you to settle for the available insurance coverage. We run asset searches on defendants where a policy limit is likely to be reached. This way, our clients have a

better idea on the possibility of collecting a judgment over the insurance policy.

2. They failed to present the full scope of your injuries to the defendant.

3. They advised settlement because they failed to prepare your case.

Settlements are serious business. They are the final resolution of all your claims against a defendant. Know your rights.

Low Insurance / No Insurance Defendants

Low Insurance

One of the worst conversations that I have with someone who has been severely injured is telling them that the person who harmed them has a minimum policy. I wish lawmakers had to tell folks with tens or hundreds of thousands of dollars of medical bills that the most they'll receive from the person who wronged them is $20,000.

Here are the minimum insurance policies in Connecticut:

1. $20,000 for injury to or death of a person,

2. $40,000 for injury to or death of more than one person in any accident, and

3. $10,000 for property damage (CGS §§ 38a-335 and 14-112(a)).

In today's world, a single ER trip can cost $20,000. These low limits are just wrong.

No Insurance

The only thing worse than a low insurance policy is when the person who hits you has no insurance. Your only option is likely to make a claim against your own policy, and this is known as an underinsured motorist (UIM) claim. In a UIM claim, your insurance policy covers the person who hit you. Your liability limits are the amount of coverage available to you.

Do I need a lawyer in order to file a UIM claim?

Most likely. Insurance companies have thousands of lawyers. They act to protect their money at all costs, and at the time you were in the accident you went from their customer to an adversary. They are going to try to pay you as little as possible.

What will your lawyer do? Your lawyer will make a claim against your insurance policy in the exact same way a claim would have been made against the person who hit you. Your lawyer will also evaluate a claim to see if the person who hit you has any assets that you can recover. Mostly people without insurance have nothing to attach, but your lawyer needs to explore this.

Sudden Emergency Theory

That brown dog. The jerk.

The brown dog is all over the pages of deposition transcripts. He's always brown, usually about 40 pounds. His breed is unclear. He's possibly part lab, maybe some terrier, we're not really sure. Whatever he looks like, he's the Bigfoot of the car accident defense world and he's been blamed for many, many car accidents.

If a car wreck is caused by some sudden emergency, a driver may not be held accountable for causing an accident. Lawyers call this the "sudden emergency doctrine." In a case where a driver has a sudden heart attack while driving, the doctrine makes sense. If a driver was having a heart attack, that driver had no way to control his vehicle.

But the dog. The dog is much woo.

Our brain is wired to protect itself. Many folks have difficulty accepting responsibility when they cause harm to others. The brain wants a way out – any way out. So when an insurance company interviews a client, it can plant the suggestion in his client's mind by asking the question, "Did a dog jump out in front of you?"

Many times people in car accidents don't accurately remember the accident. There's a fog. In that fog may be a dog. The good news is we know how to deal with that damn dog. How? We don't chase the dog. Not for a second. A driver has an obligation to keep his eyes on the road and vehicle under control. We focus on the conduct of the driver. We do this in deposition and if necessary at trial. By the time we're done there's no doubt there was no dog. None.

Don't for a second accept the insurance company's brown dog story. That's something they created to protect their money.

Recklessness

Whenever we review a personal injury case, we investigate to see if a driver was operating recklessly. Connecticut law provides that no person shall operate any motor vehicle upon any public highway of the state recklessly, having regard to the width, traffic and use of such highway, the intersection of streets and the weather conditions.

How do we determine if a driver is reckless? We look for the following factors:

1. Was the person operating a motor vehicle while knowing or having reason to know of facts that create a high possibility of risk of physical harm to another, and yet deliberately proceeded to act in conscious disregard of, or with indifference to, that risk?

2. Was a person operating a motor vehicle while knowing or having reason to know of facts that create a high degree of risk?

3. Was the person operating a motor vehicle upon any public highway at such a rate of speed as to endanger the life of any person other than the operator of the motor vehicle?

4. Did the person operate the motor vehicle upon any public highway at a rate of speed greater than 85 miles per hour?

If any of those four factors are present, the person who caused your injuries may be responsible for reckless driving.

Reckless driving may entitle you to double or treble damages. That means two or three times the amount you would have been awarded in a wreck without reckless driving.

Reckless driving needs to be specially pleaded in a complaint.

Epilogue

Personal injury law is constantly evolving, and we work hard to stay on top of the current trends and discussions. If you are looking for additional information or a topic I may not have covered here, please check out my blog, A Connecticut Law Blog (www.aconnecticutlawblog.com). I know the legal landscape is very difficult for those who have been injured to navigate, so if you have additional questions, feel free to email me at ryan@cttrialfirm.com or call me at 860-471-8333.

The purpose of this book is to empower those wrongfully injured by giving them the knowledge they need to understand the circumstances they face. I know that we cannot take every case. We cannot right every wrong. I hope this book has better helped you understand Connecticut personal injury law.

Thank you.

Ryan
March 2018

Glossary

Brief – a written legal argument that an attorney will file with the court in order to assist a judge in making a decision. Briefs are commonly filed in support of or in objection to a motion.

Defendant – a person defending a lawsuit.

Deposition – sworn, out-of-court testimony by a witness or a party to a lawsuit that is normally transcribed or videotaped for use in court.

Law – a nexus of statutes, regulations, rules, and court or agency decisions. When someone says, "It's the law," that person could be referring to any one of these sources or to a few in combination. For example, statutes and court decisions interpreting those statutes must be read together in order to fully understand the current state of the law.

Motion – a request for the court to take a particular action.

Plaintiff – a person who is bringing a lawsuit.

www.ingramcontent.com/pod-product-compliance
Lightning Source LLC
Chambersburg PA
CBHW060024210326
41520CB00009B/985